CHRISTOPHER

WHERE TO FIND A

WARM BUCKET

and other

TALL TALES of a LOW PLACE

Designed and edited by Carol and Martin Carman
Typing by Janet South

Warm Bucket

First published in 2019 by McCaw Press

ISBN: 978-0-9930130-3-4

An address for McCaw Press can be found via the 'Contact Us' section of the website http://www.dennisofgruntyfen.co.uk/shop/
or email info@dennisofgruntyfen.co.uk

For more about Grunty Fen,
including recordings and memorabilia,
please visit www.dennisofgruntyfen.co.uk

Printed and bound in Great Britain by Impressions Print and Label, Somersham, Huntingdon PE28 3EE

What the critics say about

Warm Bucket

'South's heroic insouciance in the face of vile phenomena
is almost preternatural'
The New Gutter

'An unblinking and even-handed account
of the absolutely disgusting'
Plasterer and Pargetter Monthly

'Not for the timid or faint-hearted'
Rugger Thuggery

'Not since Amazon explorers met tribes unknown to civilization
have we heard such astounding travellers' tales'
British Xylophone incorporating Modern Glockenspiel

'Full'
The Quantity Surveyor

'A bucket of fun for everyone!'
The Amateur Embalmer

'You don't know how long I've waited for this book'
The Editor

By the same author and available from www.dennisofgruntyfen.co.uk

The Authorised Guide to Grunty Fen

'Like a modern Marco Polo, the intrepid Mr South has made startling discoveries in an almost unknown region'
The Sightseer

'Makes paying an actual visit quite unnecessary or, indeed, desirable'
The East Anglian Wayfarer

Who's Who in Grunty Fen

'This work widens the scope of biography'
Dorothy Long

'There has never been anything like it'
Prince Oswald

The Customs and Folklore of Grunty Fen

'Mr South shows great courage in bringing this book to public attention and I hope it gets the reception it so richly deserves'
Rev. Dr Arnold Dicey

'The explicit scenes of sex and violence are entirely justified'
Dolores Bagmaid

'Say what you like but he works ever so hard'
Mrs South

Contents

PREFACE

HOW TO USE THIS BOOK   **1**
    Measurements and Wayfarers' Bones
    Key to Symbols

GENERAL INFORMATION ABOUT THE AREA   **4**
    The Influence of the Railways
    Hiccup Gardens
    Lost Villages
    Lost People
    The 'Seaside' and 'Wild West' Villages
    The Privies

ESSENTIAL INFORMATION   **16**
FOR TRAVELLERS ATTEMPTING THE ITINERARIES
    Bus travel
    Accommodation
    Souvenirs
    Itineraries

ITINERARIES   **30**

    Itinerary One   30
        Devil's Pittance
        Lower Grime
        The Gibbets
        The Pitts
        Rank Sumps
        Fairfen

Contents

Itinerary Two   41
Good Grief
Cruel Winter
Stalag Luft

Itinerary Three   51
Dearie Me
Gritttaketen
San Francisco
Warm Ponds
Upper and Lower Drayne

Itinerary Four   65
New Luton
East Pole
Dirty Corner

OTHER PLACES OF INTEREST   **74**
The Fortresses
The Zoo
The Great Central Swamp
    (and The Pylon People)
Retard Hall
Great Cambridge University

INDEX AND PICTURE CREDITS   At the back

This book is dedicated to the memory of Pete Sayers without whom it would have been impossible.

ACKNOWLEDGEMENTS

The Author would like to thank
Miss Edwards, Carol Carman, Martin Carman and Janet South
whose ceaseless nagging, bullying and interference
made this book what it is.

PREFACE

IT WOULD BE WRONG to claim that this latest exploration of the furthest-flung fens breaks new ground since so little of the area visited counts as true ground rather than as quaking marsh and boggy thickets. Indeed, we venture for the first time into the Great Central Swamp and discover the apparent source of the warm buckets treasured by many fen families to the point of worship.

These buckets with their constant and inexplicably warm slime serve as objects of domestic reverence. They serve also as a symbol for visitors of inexhaustible surprises and equally warm welcome awaiting credulous travellers seeking to use this little book as a guide through the barely believable territory it describes.

Dip your own bucket into this mysterious morass and meet incredible people who live there untouched by changes afflicting the rest of us. Abandon the restraints that cripple and cocoon our dull little lives to join me in a wonderful world that rises triumphantly above its superficial squalor.

Christopher South
Crass Combust
Summer 2019

MEASUREMENTS AND WAYFARERS' BONES

To help travellers immerse themselves in the rich cultural heritage of the area, we have adopted the traditional local method of navigation and calculating distances. Readers familiar with our earlier works will know that fenfolk measure journeys by indicating distances from a single fixed point, much as Oxford Circus is taken as the notional centre of London, a stone column in Nagpur as the centre of India, and the Temple of Heavenly Peace in Beijing as the centre of the universe.

Largely because it is easily the tallest and most visible structure for many miles around, the centre point of the Fens is taken to be the venerable cast-iron Stink Pipe attached to the gents behind The Bull public house at Grunty Fen. In this book, readers will find such references as SP9, SP15 or SP20 indicating, for principal places, their distance in miles from the pipe. However, in order to fix an exact location, travellers seeking absolute authenticity will need a map and a set of wayfarers' bones. In the absence of geometricians' dividers or compasses, fen folk long ago learned how to use the wishbones of various birds to span the distance between the Stink Pipe and a spot on the map. A goldcrest wishbone, for example, represents a very short distance of less than a mile, whereas a goose wishbone may take us beyond Dank and a swan's bone to the very edges of the known fens depending on the scale of the map and the size of the bird.

Very valuable sets of wayfarers' bones are heirlooms treasured by families because they include the bones of the now-extinct Great

1

Bustard, heraldic supporter of the arms of Cambridgeshire, and used by early explorers of those far-flung and mysterious reaches of the Fens from which, even now, expeditions seldom return. (See *Who's Who in Grunty Fen* p6).

So if you hear someone in a fen pub say a football team have an away fixture 'a cock robin off' or someone is courting a girl 'a pigeon away' you will understand what's meant. However, expressions using the term 'Great Bustard' should be interpreted with caution.

Fen names for otherwise unidentified birds include: the Foul Fowl, notorious for its disgusting habits; the very rare Carrion Thrush which eats its own fledglings; the Marsh Hurrier which darts about and never settles; the Homing Vulture, now extinct but once used extensively in fen tribal warfare; the Funeral Rook, whose sobbing, plaintive cry is often heard at fen obsequies; the Killer Robin whose jaunty call of 'Murder! Murder!' echoes across the marshes in spring.

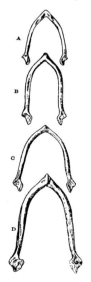

Left: Wayfarers' bones from various fen birds which show the necessity for matching the bones to the correct scale of map:

A) Lesser Bustard B) Small Bustard

C) Medium Bustard D) Great Bustard

KEY TO SYMBOLS

Terrain

Height above sea level

SP   Distance from Stink Pipe (in miles)

Pubs

Chief Industry

Warning (Important or Vital)

Estimated population

Places of worship

Places of interest

Restaurants

Principal Dangers

Points to note

3

THE INFLUENCE OF THE RAILWAYS

Visitors are often puzzled to find many fen villages have one or more terraced houses named Railway Cottages, even when no railway has ever come within several miles. There is even a Railway Inn at Slug Fen although the nearest railway line was eight miles away and closed in the 1960s. What that pub and all those Railway Cottages have in common is a curiously rectilinear quality, whereas in general, despite the rigidity of corrugated iron, fen architecture has a casual, curvilinear style.

At times the almost haphazard use of found materials makes it hard to tell where a building ends and the fen begins; cottages seem to emerge bearing traces of leafy loam. But these mysterious Railway Cottages have stark horizontals and verticals. A close inspection tells the curious visitor why: these homes are built from materials acquired during attempts to build railways in the area in the late 19th century. Construction was greatly delayed because whole lengths of 'permanent way' were removed overnight together with the sleepers on which they were laid. Those steel rails, those stout sleepers are the invisible components of the Railway Cottages.

Perhaps the most striking example of this railway architecture is the unique tower and spire of the Chapel of Truth and Honesty at Dodge Fen which somehow escaped the eye of Nikolaus Pevsner in his Cambridgeshire volume.

HICCUP GARDENS

While exploring the rich landscape of the Fens the observant wayfarer may wonder why small hedged or fenced cultivated areas of an odd geometrical shape are found, sometimes far from any habitation or sometimes having a single modest residence surrounded by neatly tended flowers and vegetables. These are the famous Hiccup Gardens and their origin is astounding even in this land of surprises.

According to a well-attested account, the Hiccup Gardens story begins not here in the Fens but in an engineering draughtsman's offices in Darlington at the height of railway mania.

In the second half of the 19th century fortunes were made and lost in the construction of a network of tracks criss-crossing England. After the great main lines were completed, investors poured money into schemes reaching into the furthest-flung corners of the country. Then, when there was nowhere else to build, they turned to the Fens.

Here commercial opportunities were few, the population was bellicose and vast bogs gobbled up any newly-laid tracks not misappropriated by a surly citizenry (see opposite).

To make matters worse, there was a serious shortage of railway engineers to mastermind these smaller schemes. All the great names were fully engaged not only in England but throughout the Empire.

So it was that the newly formed Fenland and Anglia Oriental Steam Navigation Company engaged Makepeace Daunt Armiger, a city sewers designer whose lifetime struggle to cope with the tidal consequences of the Industrial Revolution had broken his health while earning him the nickname 'Mucky Moses', an allusion to that prophet's exploits in the Red Sea.

5

Armiger was in wretched health when he accepted the fen railway contract as a chance to get some fresh air in his lungs after years in sewer construction. He surveyed the tricky territory where the new line would run and retired to his drawing office to make a detailed plan.

Among his many medical conditions, he was wracked by hiccups so seismic that they shook his frail frame. With his new employers urging for a start on their railway, he bravely pressed on producing sheet after sheet of detailed drawings and trying to ignore massive attacks of the hiccups. Each time he endured a spasm his right hand jerked uncontrollably and while trying to draw a straight line or a gentle curve to indicate trackside fencing, he created a series of u-shaped deviations. Desperate to get the job done, he had no time to correct these accidental kinks before the track-layers snatched the drawings from his hands and set to work. As they proceeded across the fen they were accompanied by the track-fencers who faithfully fenced the 'permanent way', incorporating the hiccup kinks.

Left: The stress of years spent wrestling with vast sewerage schemes shows on the face of Makepeace Daunt Armiger who was sadly wracked by embarrassing spasms when he sought a quieter life bringing a railway to the Fens.

The whole enterprise was doomed anyway. The permanent way proved far from permanent; those few stretches completed soon subsided or were stolen. All that now remains are the u-shaped fenced-off areas beside the vanished track. Would Armiger be pleased to see how his hiccups have become a series of beautiful small gardens? Local people, taking advantage of the uncertain ownership of the u-shaped areas, quickly moved in. Hedges were planted as windbreaks. Fruit, vegetables and flowers now flourish in these pockets of fertile fen soil known as the Hiccup Gardens

Although bees are elsewhere absent from this flowerless area, a series of apiaries has arisen in the Hiccup Gardens, the hives being constructed from railway fence posts and sleepers which give the honey a distinctive tang of creosote. It is said to be a sovereign remedy for infantile croup and is used as a thoracic lubricant by local clergy before embarking on their more ambitious Lenten sermons.

Tours of these delightful horticultural spectacles can be arranged; speak to Miss Edwards at Grunty Fen Post Office Stores to book Dennis, verger of St Judas' parish church, as a guide.

Below: Fenland and Anglia Oriental Steam Navigation Company (F&O) coat of arms with motto 'Celerity cum Celery' – Speed with Celery.

Quarterly, first sable three celeries in bend argent; second argent rising sun sable in fess; third argent locomotive statant sable; fourth sable four bars wavy argent.

These Arms are registered with the Universal College of Imperial Heralds, Blight Fen Branch. All enquiries to: Lord Luigi Mendoza-Barltrop, The College of Heralds, Bloke Road, Scrap End, Dank, near Down Market, Cambs.

The word 'Oriental' in the company's title signifies the founder's intention to extend a railway or canal ultimately to link Ely, Wisbech, Cambridge and Scant with other regional centres and Scratby, which they planned to develop as an East Coast seaside resort comparable with Brighton.

LOST VILLAGES

Daily life in far-flung fens is lived out against a background of uncertainty not only of the survival of the people but of the very villages they inhabit: it is a fact of existence here that villages come and villages go.

Although documentary evidence for the lost villages is scanty, we can hazard the names and the approximate locations of dozens of vanished communities. The clues lie in their surviving neighbours.

If there is now (as there is) the village of West Rutts, it may be assumed that there was at one time a Rutts or even a North, South and East Rutts. By the same token, the existence of Lower Sluvvenleigh implies an Upper (or possibly just Low) Sluvvenleigh.

But pinpointing the exact former location of, say, West Scurfly Fen by digging experimental archaeological trenches can be a hazardous undertaking: the same fateful forces that afflicted the village in some previous century may remain active, and why risk lives seeking the remains of a village which was probably indistinguishable from its surviving neighbour? If there was hope of finding another Troy or another Machu Picchu it would be worth the effort, but another Sluvvenleigh is less persuasive.

Even so, interest in tracing lost villages is strong. A fascinating study of police missing persons files shows how dozens of metal detectorists have disappeared while surveying certain uninhabited parts where oral tradition indicates a village. The legendary Great and Little Grudge have, if police figures are to be believed, consumed seven detectorists in the past twenty years, although the true figure may be much higher because many detectorists' spouses do not, for one reason or another, report them missing.

LOST PEOPLE

Whilst dealing with things lost let us take this opportunity to mention the Lost People. Perhaps the most elusive denizens of the area, they are nomads, seldom settling anywhere for more than two or three days as they ceaselessly roam the fen seeking their lost home. They have been given the derisive nickname of 'Hutentots'.

Not only have they lost track of their old home but they have forgotten how they lost it. Many villages simply sink into the fen, but did some other disaster drive them away? Clearly they had time to remove components of their village before it vanished: men, women and children now laboriously carry corrugated iron sheeting and massive railway sleepers, re-erecting their huts and chapel wherever local people will tolerate them.

These tragic wanderers often have to endure shouts of 'Hutentots go home!' to which the anguished reply is 'But we don't know where our home is!' and the Hutentots are even uncertain of their lost home's name: some say it was Spewing-in-the-Marsh, others insist it was Slimepits – perhaps a corruption of Limepits or perhaps not.

All we can say for certain is that they have been known as the Hutentots ever since a missionary giving talks about his work in Africa some years ago referred to the Hottentots. This inspired local wags to call the wandering villagers 'Hutentots' and the name stuck.

The settled population says the Hutentots are unnatural and irreverent because they worship in only one chapel for which the ground has to be newly consecrated each time it is moved.[*]

[*] *For a basic grounding in the various religions, cults and followings in the area, see* The Authorised Guide to Grunty Fen. *See also* The Pitts, *p35 of this volume.*

9

The Hutentots' only income stems from their extraordinary manual dexterity and acute eyesight. The steady hands of the sharp-eyed ladies enable them to thread even the finest needles with the thickest threads, a task for which local ladies with their huge, clumsy fingers readily pay, often purchasing a store of threaded needles to last until the Hutentots' next visit.

Meanwhile, the Hutentot men have used their natural manual and ocular gifts to develop extraordinary veterinary skills. They can neuter any creature, great or small; ponies, donkeys, pigs, cockerels, cats, dogs, goats and rabbits are all neutered so swiftly and accurately that the creature is unaware until much later. One legendary Hutentot was challenged to neuter a shrew; he not only succeeded but went on to neuter a cock wren in flight without the bird missing a wing-beat. This ability is regarded by their clients with apprehensive awe. They admire and employ the Hutentots to neuter their stock but are always at pains to pay in full and promptly 'for fear of upsetting them'.

As we warned at the outset, the Hutentots are elusive and your chances of spotting their portable village at a transitory site or even in transit are slim. In a high wind the rattling and clanking of corrugated iron sheets may give you a clue; the same sheets when dragged to a new site sometimes gouge a rut in soft turf but it is hard to be sure in which direction the Hutentots were moving.

One way of contacting them is to mention that you have an animal to be neutered. They may come to you, but you will have to provide an animal and be ready to pay promptly to avoid unfortunate retaliatory action.

Above: A rare picture of a typical Hutentot dwelling. Held together with a few rudimentary fixings, it can be dismantled at a moment's notice.

THE 'SEASIDE' AND 'WILD WEST' VILLAGES

Newcomers are sometimes startled by signposts to such places as Ilfracombe, Southwold and Shanklin or to Apache Wells, Calamity Gulch and Tombstone City.

Sadly, these settlements have long since vanished if they ever existed and the signs are mute memorials to the ambition of Billy 'Butlin' Dyke, one of a fen family famous as entertainment entrepreneurs. It was Billy's sister, Chenille, who founded the celebrated Museum of Salad Cream Bottles that was once a great draw at Festering-in-the-Heaps holiday village.[*]

In the 1950s, Billy saw holiday camp potential in the murky pools left behind by the 19th-century coprolite industry.[**] Due to the uncertain ownership of these pools, Billy was, with Chenille, able to include them in an ambitious scheme for a chain of small family holiday camps with self-catering chalets made from Anderson air-raid shelters then freely available.

Billy, a keen cinemagoer, named several projected camps after Western film locations, and his sister named others after English seaside resorts that she hoped to be able to afford to visit if their scheme succeeded.

Unfortunately a poorly worded advertising campaign led to potential holidaymakers' responses being delivered to Apache Wells in Arizona, Shanklin on the Isle of Wight, etc. to the mystification of the recipients.

---

[*]*The collection is presently in the East Anglian Museum of Cultural Curiosities and Mouth Organs at 27c Chimney Street, Great Yarmouth.*

12

Left: A weather-beaten fingerpost points poignantly to where the 'Cornish' range of air-raid shelters once awaited holidaymakers.

Right: A rusting sign is all that remains of Billy 'Butlin' Dyke's plans for a Wild West holiday camp.

**Coprolite, fossilised dinosaur dung, was excavated at many fenland sites for use as a phosphate-rich plant food. The quarries were soon worked out or were supplanted by cheaper sources of fertiliser.*

13

THE PRIVIES

Scattered across a wide area of the Fens are a number of villages bearing variations of the word 'privy' in their names. Chill Pryvy, for example, or Privie Marshland, Dry Privy and even the curious Sticky Privy.

The names bring much mockery upon the residents, and a union of Women's Institutes from the Privy villages went so far as to publish a somewhat spurious historical leaflet seeking to explain that Privy, Pryvie, Privie, etc. are all corruptions of *privet*, the evergreen shrub widely planted as domestic hedging in select suburbs. The ladies even had a campaign of mass privet planting to secure their 'true' status and origins.

Sadly, the truth is otherwise and rather more interesting. What Dashfor Privy, Water Privey, Fowl Pryvie, Privie Locknot and all the others joined by name have in common is the work of the 19th-century hygiene movement led by The Society for Sanitary Reform among the Labouring Classes, founded by Lady Louise ('Lulu') Sapper-Trench. Lulu (or, as some have it, Loo-Loo) was a persuasive fund-raiser and soon had enough money to pay for public water closets to be installed in a dozen fen villages which had for centuries managed without.

However, she met with stubborn resistance from the very people she was trying to help. Vocal opponents told Lady Louise '…what you can do with your buckets'. Undeterred, the good lady proceeded to build conveniences, slightly less conveniently in open country outside villages but accessible if the user set out in good time. Slowly the local people were won over and saw the merits of modern sanitation.

By this time Lady Louise had run out of funds and could not move the lavatories back into villages. As a consequence, there arose a steady stream of young couples building their first homes and the elderly with gastro-urinary problems settling into housing near the privies. In time the clusters of houses around the privies grew into independent hamlets and villages and were considered desirable 'up-market' areas.

Even now 'I'm off to see Lady Lulu' is a common fen euphemism for going to the lavatory. But the belief that the modern use of 'loo' derives from 'Lulu' is no more convincing than attributing 'Privy' to privet.

Above: One of the original 'Lady Lulu' toilets, now restored and exhibited at the Guild of Sanitary Inspectors' Hall in the City of London.

ESSENTIAL INFORMATION
FOR TRAVELLERS ATTEMPTING THE ITINERARIES

BUS TRAVEL

In those areas served by roads, local bus services are highly recommended but not as a means of getting about. The routes and even the destinations of most buses are so arbitrary and open to alteration to cope with changing circumstances or commercial opportunities that they seldom offer a sensible or practical option to the serious traveller whose time is precious. But local buses do offer an irresistible chance to glimpse or even become part of local life.

Any journey is a magical mystery tour and seeking the driver's guidance can be like consulting the Delphic Oracle. Finding it hard to read the words pencilled on a fragment of corrugated cardboard wedged under a bus windscreen wiper, one tourist asked if this was indeed the bus for Windy Huts. The one-word reply, although expressed in the most civil tone, was 'Depends.' Pressed for detail, the driver, one Nigel, said his departure and route depended 'on Mrs Starling's contractions.' However, the lady's waters had not yet broken and although Mrs Starling had been in labour for many hours, the bus might not be needed to take her to the Cottage Hospital until Mr Starling came home and she could get tea ready.

But surely the Cottage Hospital had an ambulance? Naturally, said Nigel, but it had taken the Over-60s to the seaside and would not be back until late afternoon.

Thus does public transport proceed in the Grunty Fen area and almost no-one grumbles because every journey is packed with interest and incident.

The single cause for complaint is that the staff's sidelines crowd out potential passengers. For example, Nigel has invested in a double-decker so that he can use the top deck as a hatchery for his bantam chicks or for propagating pansies, petunias and other basic bedding plants for sale in the spring. Nigel finds the heat from passengers on the lower deck suits his seedlings and cigarette smoke wafting up the stairs deters aphids.

At other times he rents out the same space to a travelling corsetiere, a palmist, a small-animals vet and a lady expert in herbal remedies for a range of sexually transmitted diseases. This means that the lower deck must accommodate all passengers, their ducks, geese and other livestock, luggage and tools of their trades – shotguns, scythes, saws, sickles and slashers all becoming entangled

Above: Nigel's bus being dug out of soft soil after a consignment of sugar beet broke loose, unbalancing the weight distribution and causing him to swerve violently and run off the road.

17

with mothers and their toddlers' trikes, missionaries and their portable pulpits, fen landscape painters with their easels and, in the early evening, the high-spirited trainee chimney sweeps burdened by equipment for their homework after a busy day on the Calcified Carboniferous Flue and Gaseous Effluvium course at Down Market College of Vocational Fine Arts. A ride is a course in itself, presenting a colourful tapestry of fen life as the fortunate stranger journeys he knows not whither, for Nigel improvises his route to match the needs of his passengers or any unexpected events along the way.

Here a widow flags down the bus because she needs Nigel's help to empty her heavy closet bucket. A little further on, his finger is needed to hold a knot while a pensioner parcels up a birthday present of good fen carrots for her granddaughter who has emigrated to Bedfordshire. And then the bus is diverted along a little-used lane for an emergency delivery of inner tubes to a stranded cyclist. The bus is further delayed while Nigel opens the lid of a jar of piccalilli for a young woman whose husband is away from home during the rhubarb harvest.

His route is further complicated by Nigel's courteous insistence on dropping off his clients as close to their homes as dyke, mire and obstructive vegetation permit. At each stop passengers pay fares in goods rather than money: small sacks of carrots, heads of celery, duck eggs, pigeon squabs, cheese muffins, and bottles of elderberry wine accumulate in the driver's cab.

For the visitor, such a bus ride is an unforgettable experience but, alas, even Nigel's bus is beyond the reach of many communities which lack anything a city dweller would call a road. Thorny thickets thrive in the rich marsh mud and defy the ceaseless labours of local men to hack out and maintain a link to the outside world. Such is the vigour of this poisonous greenery that it quickly closes in again behind those trying to tame it and a track becomes impenetrable once more. Here, walking or wading have for centuries been the only means of getting about. An evening stroll can require the use of a blade like the Nepalese Kukri or the knife used by sugarcane harvesters.

But between the bus routes and the pedestrian swampways there is a third mode of travel. Especially in the summer months when epidemics of the Green Flux are rarer and less fatal, undertakers offer their hearses as taxis and occasionally combine the two functions by offering lifts to people who have no connection to the deceased but are going the same way. If as a tourist you try this means of transport then you will be asked to avoid upsetting the bereaved by laughing or smiling. You will also be asked as far as possible to hide behind a wreath or other floral tribute.

Right: On the bus you may be lucky enough to meet one of the 'high-spirited trainee chimney sweeps burdened by equipment for their homework after a busy day on the Calcified Carboniferous Flue and Gaseous Effluvium course at Down Market College of Vocational Fine Arts'.

ACCOMMODATION

With the exception of the Interrogation Suite mentioned in our section on Stalag Luft (p48), no accommodation is available in any of the points of call in our suggested itineraries. There are, however, a number of S&B (sofa and breakfast) houses conveniently placed as bases for travellers planning to take their time. See pp22-23 for details.

Perhaps the most palatial accommodation available to visitors is Her Majesty's Pleasure Hotel on a stretch of open fen just outside Dry Bicker.

When the Home Office first purchased this site for a new prison for sex-murderers they had in mind not only its remoteness from civilization but also the fact that Dry Bicker residents were unlikely to complain; a high proportion of Dry Bickerers have always helped keep Chelmsford, Highpoint, Littlehey and Bedford jails busy. As was hoped, there were no local objections to the sex-murderers joining the community.

However, before the first brick had been laid there was a radical change of Home Office policy to cope with a drastic shortage of open prisons for big business embezzlers who had defrauded millions of pensioners, and Members of Parliament who had accepted huge bribes from enemies of the state to disclose security and commercial information or to vote in ways directed by their paymasters abroad.

Outrage swept through Dry Bicker on hearing that they were to have crooked politicians as neighbours.

'We say no to human vermin,' declared Parish Council chairlady Mrs Victoria Abbs.

'This is a decent village,' said the Rev. Morris Lambert. 'We don't want this scum here.'

'Bring back hanging for bent MPs,' said the Over-60s.

'Sex-criminals in there? Cool,' said the Youth Club. 'Lying, cheating, two-faced, grasping politicians? Not cool.'

Faced with such a barrage of opposition the Home Office, which had meanwhile built the open prison, was eventually forced to abandon it. The cells intended for multi-millionaire embezzlers and venal legislators now form two suites worthy of the Ritz and are available for the most demanding tourist.

Sadly, Her Majesty's Pleasure has a poor reputation for the safeguarding of guests' small, moveable valuables but the rooms are comfortable. The restaurant, The Thieves' Kitchen, is commodious and The Bar Behind Bars is popular with locals and visitors alike.

This space has been left blank for your own notes.

Madame Flo Wragg

takes in anyone at her

ACADEMY OF DANCE AND THE THESPIAN ARTS

B&B&B (banquette, breakfast and ballet class)

Special arrangements for gentlemen tap dancers

Free paso doble demonstration every day 9-10 am
(except Good Friday)

Share towel. Bring own castanets and roller-skates.

8, THE HARD GRIND, BLUDD

The Hornet Tattoo and Massage Parlour

1-19 Back Street, Dense.

Comfortable couches, flask refill, free rub down and
simple hornet tattoo on any body part (except elbow).
No catering but on a good fish and chip van route.

SLURRYBANK COTTAGE, HARROWING

Mrs Scrubbs offers S&B and optional evening meal.
(*Please bring own cutlery and cruet.*)

THE ROYAL GENTRY RITZ PLAZA

formerly Hilton Park Palace Hotel
***** Spitehaven Tourist Board Rating

> ➤ Comfortable (three-piece) suites in both front room and scullery.

> ➤ Self-catering but help given with range. Kindling extra.

> ➤ Fully licentious.

17, The Front, Spitehaven   *No Portuguese.*

Mesdames Daisy Swaffield and Jo Banks
have ample accommodation
for individuals or large parties
at
The Smallholding
Scrape's End, Wrasp

during the summer months
when the goats are out to pasture.
(No vegetarians or Nazis.)

SOUVENIRS

The infant tourist industry in the Grunty Fen area has already encouraged local people to fulfil a growing demand for mementoes reflecting their rich cultural heritage. So far, these souvenirs fall into three categories: **delicacies**, **handicrafts** and **fertilisers**.

 *Delicacies*

Women's Institutes have worked together to provide roadside stalls plus a tea room (see p74) laden with a mouthwatering range of dishes for which they are famous.* (Caution: before buying please read the warning opposite.)

Brawn Horns: These are reject pastry cases from the nearby Fancies Factory, filled with delicious pork brawn made by the ladies of the W.I. using pig heads imported in containers from Poland and set in special brawn buckets.

Spam Pasties: Do not be deterred by complaints that Spam Pasties are not what they used to be. True, the 1943 and 1944 Spam found in scattered concrete pillboxes after World War II have long been unavailable except for huge sums on the black market. But the same local herbs (Devil's Bladderwort, Deadman's Daisies and Bitter Frogspite) are used and the pasties are as savoury as ever. Cans of the modern product are a perfectly acceptable substitute.

For more information about local delicacies, please see The Authorised Guide to Grunty Fen.

Road Kill Pie: One of the unique features of RKP, as it is popularly known, is that no pie tastes exactly the same as another. Flavour and texture depend on what has been run over, generally at night, on the A10 or other busy roads.[*]

Pheasant, hare, rabbit and weasel are commonplace constituents but lucky visitors find a more exotic RKP embracing badger, hedgehog or some of the smaller vermin. Fragments of toad or even newt can be surprisingly succulent but purchasers of an RKP generally prefer not to ask what is in it. An eminent Cambridge zoologist once dissected an RKP and quipped that he found 'species unknown to science!'

 IMPORTANT WARNING: Wise tourists buy their pies from the Women's Institutes' outlets rather than from other informal roadside vendors with no guarantee of quality.

The W.I. abide by their own equivalent of the sell-by date system found elsewhere. You will find written on the bag or newspaper in which your W.I. RKP is wrapped a message such as 2BIGO or 1BIGO. This indicates the number of days a pie may be kept Before It Goes Off. The W.I. ladies vary their calculations to match weather conditions and on hot days your RKP may be as little as ½ BIGO.

[*]*For details of the economic importance of gleaning from the A10 see* The Customs and Folklore of Grunty Fen.

 *Handicrafts*

Local handicrafts are always popular potential tourist souvenirs.

Whittled whisks and whistles: Full details of these ingenious contrivances are given on p32 in our section on Lower Grime but whittled whisks and whistles are also occasionally available elsewhere. Keep your eyes open but be careful to avoid chapped or swollen lips from an unseasoned whittled whistle. Unseasoned whittled whisks are safe but will taint whatever is whisked, especially champagne.

Eelskin shoe laces: Since nylon laces were introduced, eelskin shoe and boot laces have become rarer but are worth seeking out if only for their entertainment value. It was a visiting Victorian clergyman, Eustace Growner, who described trying to lace his boots with eelskin as 'akin to threading a bodkin with an earthworm' and it is surprising how lively eelskin laces are. Sometimes they almost tie themselves but when in a contrary mood the same laces will suddenly untie themselves and leave the wearer stumbling slipshod into a ditch where the laces are revived by water and then defy all attempts to re-tie them.

The use of eelskin bootlaces has been the cause of many amusing incidents on the football field, especially in damp weather when opposing players' laces may tie each other in knots during close tackles. Similar scenes occur in crowded chapels when worshippers find themselves bound together in ranks of six or more and many illicit love affairs have been exposed when the parties have needed help to be parted.

For further uses of eelskin in the fields of transport and nutrition, see *Who's Who in Grunty Fen* pp52-53.

Fly hats: These clever contrivances are cheap, available almost everywhere and serve as a wonderful reminder of your days out on the fens. Men and women wear their own fly hats from freshly cut withy or willow twigs, and it is impressive to see the delicate fingers of a young woman or the sturdy digits of a working man deftly make themselves a new hat faithfully following the traditional designs. These simple wicker shapes are then immersed in a vat of glutinous and secret concoction; the stink subsides as the hat sets but remains tacky. It is then ready to wear and soon proves its worth by trapping myriad flies, wasps, bees, mosquitos and every sort of flying thing in its sticky substance leaving the lucky wearer fly-free.

It is a pity that this element of folk dress is seldom seen in today's go-ahead fen villages but fly hats still serve as a valid reminder of a great cultural tradition. A scraper to remove the accumulated insects is provided free with each hat and the scrapings are said to be a potent fertiliser for conservatory plants.

 Fly hats are recommended if travelling to within 5 miles of Cruel Winter (see p45).

Ladies' Evening Buckets: Owners of beautifully decorated traditional ladies' buckets are reluctant to part with them, especially the treasured evening buckets which are sometimes handed down through generations. But tourists stand a better chance of acquiring a beautiful although less exotic ladies' morning bucket, ladies' football bucket, a stylish bingo bucket or the more prosaic shopping bucket. Ask around. Or why not buy a blank bucket and decorate your own? It would amaze your friends!

Knitted triangles: The outcome of a drive to generate interest in handicrafts in fen schools, the knitting campaign has had limited success in a technical sense but has been amply rewarded in drawing income from tourists.

The original intention was that each child should, in the course of his or her primary school career, knit one complete square in plain stitch measuring six-by-six inches. Dropped stitches have cast a perpetual shadow over this worthy endeavour. Most pupils have, by the time they leave school, completed a whole or the greater part of a somewhat lopsided triangle; they aspired to a square but term after term lost stitches along the way. However, it is fair to say that many do achieve a wavy oblong. The organisers had intended to have squares stitched together into attractive patchwork quilts to raise money for toilet paper and other little luxuries in primary schools; as it is, the triangles are offered as pennants or any other use requiring a woolly triangle such as bikinis and the needs of the pole-dancing industry.

 Only exceptional pupils with both reading and writing go on to secondary education.

Fertilisers

Every fen village is proud of the horticultural power in the sediment which accumulates in its football team bath by the end of a season. The sediment is shovelled out, dried and sold in various sizes of packets for use in flower and vegetable gardens. The gigantic marrows, carrots, beans and pumpkins for which fen horticultural shows are famous are largely attributable to this rich sludge.

Grunty Fen Academicals sporting residues are considered best for leeks, Rat Fen Thistles F.C. for parsnips, Windy Huts Rovers for sweet peas and ladies wishing to grow mustard and cress on a kitchen windowsill are advised to use just a pinch of Dry Bicker Wednesday.

ITINERARIES

For the benefit of tourists I have drawn up four itineraries which will give merely a taste of the rich and varied life flourishing in the Fens.

❗ IMPORTANT WARNING: These itineraries start overleaf, and it should be noted that all information is correct at time of printing. However, earth movements before or during a trip may render any or all such information useless. Every journey in the Fens is undertaken at the traveller's own risk and neither the author nor the publishers can be held responsible for any deviation from the situation which presents itself to the traveller on arrival at a location.

Our companion volumes *The Authorised Guide to Grunty Fen, Who's Who in Grunty Fen* and *The Customs and Folklore of Grunty Fen* are available from all good bookshops and from www.dennisofgruntyfen.co.uk[*]

[*]*A map of Grunty Fen is also available but, whilst beautifully illustrated, it will be of no help whatsoever to the traveller.*

♦ Itinerary One ♦

Devil's Pittance – Lower Grime – The Gibbets – The Pitts –
Rank Sumps – Fairfen

This page is blank for you to draw your own map of the route.

DEVIL'S PITTANCE

☁ ❄ *Variable*	🏔 *1ft*	**SP** *13 – 25*
🏕 *32*	🙏 *33*	👁 *0*
🍺 *The Good Riddance*	🍴 *None*	
✗ *Baler twine recycling*	☠ *Local brew*	

To say this charming hamlet has no places of interest scarcely does justice to Devil's Pittance. On fine days the women sit in the sun outside their front doors (or the quaint flaps torn from tarpaulins that serve as doors), their deft fingers working swiftly to weave, knit and crochet various items such as carrot sacks, fishing nets and string vests from the stout orange plastic baler twine left over under the agricultural subsidy system. On request Mrs Gridley at No.7 will weave a bespoke ladies' evening sack for a modest gratuity.

Despite its 33 places of worship (including a rare Zoroastrian funerary tower) the hamlet has no buildings of architectural merit although Mrs Gridley is proud of her art deco coal bunker converted from a hotel reception desk left by the floods of 1947.

Devil's Pittance's sole public house, The Good Riddance, brews its own beer from the rich local water which flows behind and occasionally through the building.

! **IMPORTANT WARNING**: The Good Riddance's distance from modern medical provision makes a tasting of the local brew inadvisable.

LOWER GRIME

🐛 👣 *Up and down*   🏔 *2ft – 2ft 6in*   **SP** *11 direct, 41 by road*

👥 *320*   🙏 *2*   👁 *1*

🍺 *The Whistler's Lips (closed)*   🍴 *The Pucker Pieshop*

⚒ *Whitewood wooden whisk- and whistle-whittling*   ☠ *Whistler's lips and lisp*

Lower Grime is in the throes of an industrial revolution. Pollution has turned public opinion against plastic and this has revived Lower Grime's ancient artisanal industry: wooden whisks and whistle whittling. Unfortunately, the very success of the enterprise has made it difficult for Grimer whistle-whittlers to explain their craft to visitors owing to a common speech defect.

Like the whittled whisks, the whistles are whittled from white elder wood which naturally has a soft core; this core may be removed to form a tube. Hitherto, the craftsmen have dried the wood for up to

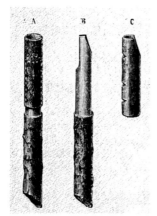

a year after removing the sap but such has been the demand to replace plastic whistles that the whittlers have been rushing their product to market with dire results for their elocution.

Left: Diagram showing the three stages of whittling a whitewood whittled whistle:

A) whipping B) whopping C) wholloping

It is well known that newly cut young elder stems have a bitter, acrid sap. This sap in an immature whistle can inflame the whistler's lips causing them to swell and making it impossible to say anything clearly, particularly the words 'whittle', 'whistle' and 'whisk'.

The whisk-whittling families are not affected in this way. They use sharp knives to partially pare thin layers of wood at one end of an immature elder stick until a sort of wooden chrysanthemum results; dipped in dyes, they can in fact be used as artificial flowers. However, unless a drying period then follows, the lingering sap taints whatever one whisks with a whitewood whittled whisk.

Choosing a piece of whitewood to be whittled into a whitewood whittled whisk is a skill in itself; the stem must be sturdy enough to withstand the whittling.

An airy whittled-whisk- or whittled-whistle-drying shed stands behind every whittler's home and all families have rights of whistlage or whiskage established in medieval times to take their raw materials from the unique elder plantations which surround the village, giving it an unmistakable rank stench.

It is a sobering thought that although Lower Grime's famed *Environmentally Sustainable Whittled Whitewood Whisks* grace the finest hotel champagne cocktail bars in the world, the village has no pub of its own and, so far as can be told, none of the whisk-whittlers or, indeed, the whistle-whittlers, has ever tasted champagne.

THE GIBBETS

Sticky   -1ft – 1ft   **SP** *It depends*

81   43   1

17   **Brasserie du Canard Flambé aux Deux Jambeaux**

Soup and stock cubes   *Entrail-related accidents*

The Gibbets' stark name, conjuring images of murderers' corpses hanging from gallows, is due entirely to the corruption of its original – The Giblets. For generations families here have been engaged in boiling and rendering down slaughtered fowl giblets imported from poultry industry centres over a wide area. At the end of the process, blocks of solidified thick giblet stock are cut into convenient cubes for cooks under the brand name Chicky-Chunks.

There is little risk of travellers failing to find their way to The Gibbets because daily deliveries in open tanks tend to slop on rough roads leaving a tell-tale entrail trail easily followed by the stranger. Travellers downwind of the rendering vats benefit from another inescapable clue to the right path.

The place of interest is the Chapel of the Demonic Druids built in the form of Stonehenge using marine ply shuttering from an abandoned drainage scheme. This remarkable edifice must have been magnificent when first completed but now suffers sadly from the failure of pebble dash to adhere to plywood sections.

THE PITTS

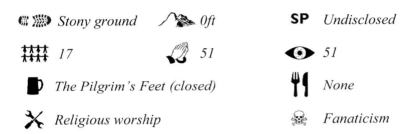

🐾 Stony ground	🏔 *0ft*	**SP**	*Undisclosed*
👥 *17*	🙏 *51*	👁	*51*
🍺 *The Pilgrim's Feet (closed)*		🍴	*None*
⚒ *Religious worship*		☠	*Fanaticism*

It is not unusual to find fen villages where the number of places of worship exceeds the number of residents but The Pitts vies with Pious End to claim the title for most religious community.

The Pitts is essentially a monastic settlement of chaste monks and nuns. This tiny but zealous band of the hooded and holy have taken a solemn vow to maintain all the chapels, churches, bethels, temples, synagogues, basilicas, mosques, stupas and gopurams experimented with by generations of their forebears before they finally settled on their present practice of Tibetan Buddhism.

They elect a different spiritual leader each day of the week, known as the Daily Lama, who guides them in the endless task of maintaining the dozens of consecrated structures in the parish.

They depend entirely on visitor donations not only to carry out this work

Right: Because of their shape, stupas are prone to being overrun by the virulent plant Strangler's Spire Throttle (epiglottis gulletitis extinguisium).

but also for their food so please be generous. You may be invited to finance the construction of an oratory where prayers for your soul will be said in perpetuity. Keen amateur photographers sometimes pay a small fee for witnessing a ritual scarification.

 Visitors may hear the sound of children reciting the Rosary but their existence is always denied.

Above: The 'Golden Galloper' village sign, unique to Fairfen. (see p.38).

RANK SUMPS

🐾 *Lonely*   🏔 *4in*   **SP** *Quite a few*

2   🙏 *0*   👁 *0*

🍺 *The Crown and Anchorite (closed)*   🍴 *None*

✗ *Loneliness*   ☠ *Loneliness*

Our visit to this modest parish can seem somewhat disappointing after the spectacular excitements of The Pitts but here we find peace and quiet away from the pious hurly-burly.

Although the official population is stated to be two persons, their gender has never been established and it is some years since either of them has been seen; they are believed to be anchorites leading a hermitic existence. The only firm evidence for their continued occupation of two huts is that well-intentioned visitors who leave alms in the form of, say, a Mars bar or a packet of Smarties, report that their gift vanishes within minutes. Cynics attribute this phenomenon to the local vermin but you may wish to give the hermits the benefit of the doubt and leave, as I did, a tube of chilli Pringles from your rucksack before setting forth on the last lap of this expedition to Fairfen.

FAIRFEN

🦶 Slimy   ⛰ -6in   **SP** *Not too far*

⛺ 122   🙏 1   👁 31

🍺 *The Merry Maggot*   🍴 *Maggotdonald's (closed)*

✕ *Maggots*   ☠ *Nasally induced nausea*

Do not let its name deceive you. If the visitor to Fairfen is expecting a fair place of roses and peaceful pastures then this intriguing new settlement will disappoint. But to an open-minded visitor marvelling at the diversity and resourcefulness of the human mind and hand this is a rich experience.

Fairfen was founded in 1992 when Gudgeon's Super Colossal Fun Fair arrived to overwinter in an area of uninhabited wasteland between Rank Sumps and Devil's Pittance. During that winter Ma Gudgeon, the matriarch of the fair family, died in a residential hotel in Hove. After minimal mourning, her multitudinous family fell to quarrelling about inheritance and it soon became clear that the business was deeply in debt, its ageing and rickety sideshows and rides being the only assets. None of the quarrelling cousins was ever again seen at the site and the equipment stood idle and open to all weathers until the following winter when fen folk living in cramped quarters came from neighbouring villages – and from as far afield as Rat Dyke, Gloat, Slutt and Good Thrashing – and began to make homes in the abandoned funfair.

The Drudge family from Snare took over the dodgems, the

Bustards from Dry Guttering installed themselves in the rifle range and the roll-a-penny sideshow was settled by the Grinders from Weeping St Less. By throwing a huge tarpaulin over the swing boats the entire Craven clan from Lower Dregs made themselves a commodious accommodation complete with hammocks. One by one the sideshows and the rides were claimed by eager squatters with perhaps the mightiest mansion, the Golden Galloper carousel, secured by the Cursed clan from Wretch and Writhing-cum-Wheary. Mrs Enid Cursed subsequently set up a successful laundry with the ability to turn her washing lines to always catch the sun and a drying breeze.

The last colonist at the new village was the Very Rev. Thrussell Fearful, founding and only priest in the Strict Perditionists for Paradise, who had his epiphany upon seeing the still-vacant helter-skelter. He rose upon the instant from being despised as the only fen religious leader with no church or chapel to having the finest steeple for miles around. During your visit you may well hear this powerful preacher calling the faithful to prayer from the top of the helter-skelter like a muezzin from a minaret.

During your visit to Fairfen take time to look closely at the scene. Engulfed in ivy, bellbind, woodbine, mildew and mosses, some sideshows are barely visible until you spot a garish sign saying 'Ghost Train' or 'Cake Walk' peeping through the leaves. It is a pity that, repelled by the unpleasant odour, visitors seldom linger to explore Fairfen more thoroughly. But, as the saying has it, where's there's muck, there's money and Fairfen's thriving maggot-breeding industry serves anglers throughout the region and beyond. The village claim theirs is a strain of maggot irresistible to even the pickiest trout; the strain was named Elizabeth Maggots as a tribute to Her Majesty.

The Bustard family in particular are proud of their maggot

clientele and offer a worldwide postal service. A sign over their office lays claim to being Maggot Breeders by Appointment to the late Queen Mother, who was a keen angler, and to her cousin, Queen Wilhelmina of the Netherlands. The Bustards still post a parcel of royal maggots to The Hague on the old Queen's birthday every year 'out of respect'. Their archives feature scores of letters from the Dutch palace but, as a proud Bustard admitted, 'We don't know what they say because we don't speak Flem.'

Above: The Bustards' maggot sheds provide not only upper and lower floors for rotation of breeding maggots but also on-site accommodation for the duty maggot-wrangler. The design is believed to have influenced the way chalets are built in Switzerland where maggot breeding is still in its infancy.

♦ ITINERARY TWO ♦

Good Grief (with view of Isolation Hospital) –
Cruel Winter – Stalag Luft

 Take stout shoes to explore this challenging but richly rewarding tour of a seldom-visited area.

This page is blank for you to draw your own map of the route.

GOOD GRIEF

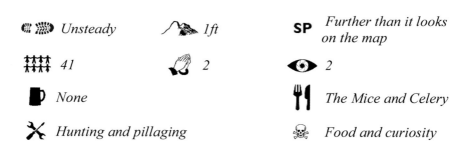

Legend has it that Good Grief got its name from the words of the explorer who first found it. (See also Dearie Me p52.)

Of ancient origin, Good Grief is locked in a time-warp and resistant to change; the people live chiefly by hunting and by pillaging celery farms to which they travel miles by night.

Since a well-wisher gave the community a wireless permanently tuned to a West London pirate radio station, the people of Good Grief have developed a language based chiefly on Jamaican reggae rap incomprehensible even to Jamaicans except for the two words 'mice' and 'celery'. Visitors may put these people at their ease by saying 'Thunny mice' as a greeting and 'Thunny celery' as a farewell.

Good Grief boasts two chapels devoted respectively to mice and celery. Before you leave you may be pressed to buy one or more mice stuffed with celery. You will be expected to use these delicacies as votive offerings at the chapels. On no account eat or even nibble the edges of them.

 Because of the preponderance of mice and celery, politely decline any invitation to dine en famille.

VITAL WARNING: We urge travellers to heed the warning signs placed at the roadside here and make no attempt to visit the low concrete buildings visible on the distant horizon. A barbed-wire fence several miles long surrounds this site which has been a no-go area for more than three centuries. The present bunkers stand where a leper colony and bubonic plague isolation hospital were originally erected; at that time the area was deemed so remote and inaccessible that only a very few local peasants would be placed at risk. When the hospital was closed it stood empty for many years in an area which had by then, for one reason or another, become totally uninhabited.

In the 19th century it was briefly used for criminal lunatics suffering from sexually transmitted diseases and a few members of the royal family, but was next converted into a refuge for the victims of various fevers contracted in the jungles of the Empire. When the Empire disintegrated and India became independent the hospital again fell idle until requisitioned by the Ministry of Defence for a nuclear weapons experimental unit.

Later the British Government, in a trade deal with the American Government, handed over the massive nuclear bunkers to

Above: Part of the old bubonic plague isolation hospital.
Because of the various diseases which had been treated there it was deemed too dangerous to remain standing and was replaced by nuclear bunkers.

a US-based international cosmetics corporation which had previously been refused permission (by the Department of Homeland Security) to build laboratories in the US. The company usually test all their face creams, anti-ageing lotions, lip balms, sun blocks, youth serums and other dermatological beauty products here, if possible before releasing them to the public.

The tall chimney visible to the east of the main block marks the company's slaughterhouse and crematorium. Abandoned farms and villages surround the site and no-one now lives within a wide radius apart from the cosmetic scientists themselves.

However, keep your eyes peeled if you are interested in wildlife. Remarkable varieties of entomological, reptilian, amphibian, mammalian and avian species appear to flourish. Natural history experts have reported sightings of marsupial hedgehogs, feathered toads, and a wren that cries 'cuckoo'. Less reliable reports from villagers living outside this forbidden zone speak of a gigantic ape-like humanoid they call 'Doomsday Dick' who supposedly terrorises communities and eats little girls.

Left: The lookout tower is all that remains of the leper colony in Good Grief; from here warnings were shouted to unwary travellers.

CRUEL WINTER

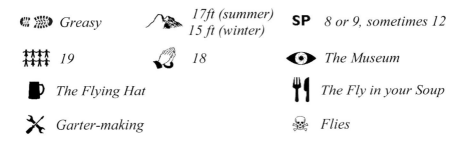

Greasy	17ft (summer) 15 ft (winter)	**SP** 8 or 9, sometimes 12
19	18	The Museum
The Flying Hat		The Fly in your Soup
Garter-making		Flies

! **IMPORTANT WARNING**: Visitors are advised to carry a good supply of insect repellent and never unwrap sandwiches, buns, toffees or pies in the parish but wait until they are at least five miles away from Cruel Winter.

At first glance, Cruel Winter may seem small and dull beside its more cosmopolitan neighbours but this straggle of ramshackle huts has a claim to fame that excels even its most cultured rivals, for in one such humble home was born a boy who became a pioneer of aviation.

Even as a lad apprenticed to the garter trade, Daniel Strippling showed commercial imagination beyond his years, proposing that eel skins could be used to make novelty surgical tourniquets. His proposal was mocked, his elders clinging to tradition, but Daniel's lively mind could not be suppressed.

It is at this point in his story that we are reminded of the young James Watt conceiving the steam engine as he watched a boiling kettle. One long, hot day spent skinning eels for garters Daniel took off his eelskin hat to mop his brow and noticed that both the hat and his brow were immediately smothered in swarms of flies. In trying to shake the flies from his hat he noticed that, contrary to all expectations, the hat seemed heavier without flies and lighter when bearing the full weight of several thousand flies. Setting it down on the ground he watched in fascination as his hat appeared to move and attempt to lift itself into the air. It was a windless day. How had his hat moved? How had his hat seemingly striven to rise without human agency?

It had to be the flies: the united efforts of a myriad tiny insects were a force with which man could conquer the air! For the rest of his long life, Daniel devoted himself to devising fly-powered aeroplanes.

He began by replacing his heavy eelskin hat with a flimsy straw hat and steadily increased the fly-power. His biggest problem was not in finding enough flies – they still proliferate throughout the area – but training the flies to behave as he wished. Time and again he would have a breakthrough with a biddable breed of fly only to be frustrated by the brevity of their existence. He tried to organise them into flights of similar age but they resisted discipline and persistently broke ranks, mingling with other flights.

Eventually he realised the only solution was to have a huge, hat-like structure made of fine, fly-proof fabric and filled with millions of flies which would be born, live and die within the 'haticopter' as he called it. Sadly, Daniel died, aged 83, before this final experiment could be completed.

He left an unpublished autobiography, *Time Flies*, in which he seeks to prove that the verb 'to fly' derives from the insect and in its first sense means 'to behave like a fly'. He also calls for a global ban on all insecticides 'by which mankind turns its back on cheap renewable powered flight'.

A small museum housing relics of his experiments, including that first eelskin hat, is Cruel Winter's only place of interest.

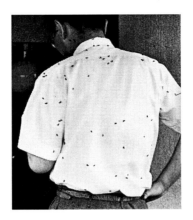

Above: As this tourist's photograph shows, flies are a perennial problem for those who choose to visit Cruel Winter.

 This space has been left blank for you to use as a fly swat.

STALAG LUFT

🍺🐾 *Interesting*   /🏔 *Classified*   **SP** *Classified*

🏃 *2-48*   🙏 *0*   👁 *1*

🍺 *None*   🍴 *The Watchtower*

✗ *Tourism*   ☠ *Rusting barbed wire*

Nothing can prepare the traveller for the shock of first sighting Stalag Luft. Unlike the almost invisible huddled huts of other fen villages which hardly break the flat horizon, Stalag Luft's grim watch-towers stand stark against the sky and, as we draw closer along Devil's Drove, we see the gothic gloom of the gatehouse. Through the cries of innumerable rooks blackening the sky we hear the clank, clank, clank of its great doors slamming in the ceaseless wintry wind. Yet pinned to the weather-worn timbers of these very gates we find written on the back of a packet of Bird's Custard Powder the words 'Welcome, Willkommen, Bienvenue' giving some clue to the present inhabitants of this fearsome fortress.

But how did a German prisoner-of-war camp come to be on this faraway fen fastness and why is a plastic palm tree visible behind the guardroom? One man, Reuben Flack, smallholder and rock-and-roll talent-spotter, holds the answers to all these mysteries.

Swine fever, fowl pest, bovine spongiform encephalitis, mange and fistulas are but a few of the calamities that befell Reuben's attempts to raise livestock on his scant acres of marsh and thorn. Nor did his arable husbandry reap better harvests. Black grass, aphids, parsnip plague, voracious celery slugs, root rot, mildew, canker, thistles and the weeping wilt afflicted his vegetables. What survived fell to pigeons and marauding crows. Somehow Reuben and his family survived on the little money he made as 'The Swiss Rocker', the world's only yodelling rock-and-roll singer. Unable to play the guitar or any other instrument, he accompanied himself on the rhythmic spoons and a tambourine in such songs of his own composing as *Fen O'Clock Rock* and the lyrical ballad *Just Walking in the Drain*. In this way he won some popularity around local nightspots where fen folk were proud to have their own star to contend with the likes of Bill Haley and The Rolling Stones. Membership of his fan club, who styled themselves the Sugar Beat Generation, soon reached the high dozens.

At one glittering venue, The Cabbage Club in Grit, he by chance bumped into Merle 'Duke' Verminstein, a film producer/director who was in search of a cheap site to build the extensive set of a major tv drama series, *Costa Esmeralda*, involving the tangled romantic affairs of young holiday-makers in a Canary Island resort. And so it came to be that a flimsy lath and plaster complex of chalets, poolside bars, dance floors and cafes sprang up where roots once rotted and poultry clucked its last. Sadly, a second series of *Costa Esmeralda* was not commissioned and the television company turned down Merle's plan for a new sitcom featuring the same set under the working title of *Prego a-go-go!* complaining that *Costa Esmeralda* had 'always looked so gloomy'.

With a year still to run of his lease on Reuben's smallholding, the resourceful film-maker saw a way to make the drawbacks of the site a virtue, and thus *Stalag Luft X*, a wartime thriller set in a Nazi prison, was born. It proved remarkably easy to convert the set since, as Merle explained, 'A cheap resort and a prison camp have a lot in common.'

Stalag Luft X ran for two series before the scores of actors and technicians finally said farewell to the fen and were soon forgotten except that they left behind a generation who were brighter and better-looking than their forebears.

The gaunt prison camp stood empty until word spread and a straggle of homeless migrants began to trickle in, which is why that custard packet on the gate is in so many languages; within the perimeter fence up to a dozen nationalities co-exist in perfect amity. Their restaurant offers a unique culinary experience ranging from borscht to bouillabaisse by way of sauerkraut, couscous and crepes. And most evenings, to the delight of diners from far and wide, Reuben moves through the happy throng yodelling rock melodies, clicking his spoons and rattling his tambourine.

 Overnight accommodation is available in the Interrogation Suite but its popularity means booking in advance.

Above: Tourists will often pay a premium to dine in one of the old watchtowers which afford a far-reaching view across the fen between the strands of barbed wire at Stalag Luft.

◆ ITINERARY THREE ◆

Dearie Me – Gritttaketen – San Francisco – Warm Ponds –
Upper and Lower Drayne

This page is blank for you to draw your own map of the route.

DEARIE ME

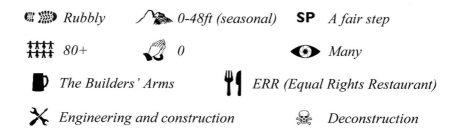

Rubbly   0-48ft (seasonal)   **SP**   A fair step

80+   0   Many

The Builders' Arms   ERR (Equal Rights Restaurant)

Engineering and construction   Deconstruction

The visitor today would hardly believe that a settlement with such miserable origins could have become the happiest village for many, many miles around. Dearie Me is held up as an example of advanced Victorian social engineering whereas its purpose was originally purely punitive or preventative detention.

Founded in 1879 by a group of wealthy Cambridge academics and clergymen, this extraordinary community was built as a nightmare oubliette for strait-laced polite society. Perpetrators of every type of sexual perversion or failure to conform to expectations might end up there; authors who wrote indecent novels, artists who carved indecent sculptures, or anyone who deviated from the path of conventional gender normality might find themselves within its boundaries.

Originally known as the Bethlehem Asylum for the Criminally Confused, it soon gained its present name because any sentence spoken about the institute always included the phrase 'Dearie me'. Every visitor was heard to sigh 'Dearie me' and even judges and magistrates committing persons there almost always muttered a valedictory 'Dearie me' as some poor wretch was led down from the dock. Parents unable to tame a weird and wilful child would weep bitter tears and sob 'Dearie me' when the trap came to take the bad boy or girl to the fenland destination spoken of only in whispers and many a 'Dearie me'.

Over the decades this human rubbish dump has developed into the brilliant centre the visitor finds today. The first thing the stranger notices, even from a distance, is the architecture of the houses and municipal buildings, but any passing resemblance to Portmeirion is misleading: all Dearie Me's strange structures are functional, practical and constantly evolving. Visit today and you will see on the skyline the unmistakable outline of several miniature Sydney Opera Houses. At the height of the fashion there were scores more but the craze is passing and nowadays replicas of the Neolithic hovels excavated at Skara Brae are increasingly seen.

Dearie Me is the only village in the vicinity to have a public library, which is housed in a reduced version of Cambridge University Library complete with 12ft tower. Elsewhere you will find versions of the Pompidou Centre, Le Corbusier's famous flats, Durham Cathedral, Anne Hathaway's Cottage and Tottenham Hotspur's stadium all in a state of construction or decline, a turmoil of change and creation.

The people (we must avoid the term 'men and women') who do all this and much more in the fields of theatre, film, sculpture, music, painting, literature, philosophy, sport, oratory, politics, medicine and the culinary arts are descended from the original population banished there in the 19th century and they perpetuate the attitudes and characteristics that landed them there. The most obvious of these traits, if not the most important, is their disregard of gender conformity. They have evolved a style of dress which makes differences imperceptible and, although marriage remains a popular formality, it covers a multitude of permutations. Outsiders who disapprove are often silenced by the fact that the birth rate at Dearie Me is more than double that of any other village in the area and possibly in the world.

The people of Dearie Me prosper by providing other less ingenious communities with cultural creations and pragmatic solutions to practical problems – it was a Dearie Me engineer who cleared High Fen drains after fifty years of stagnation.

Dearie Me people are welcomed at their neighbouring communities' social events. Hosts are at pains to put their visitors at their ease at dances by always avoiding announcing a ladies' or gentlemen's excuse-me.

Above: The abandoned building known locally as Reception because it was the waiting room for a shrine that was never built. It was meant to contain relics of holy men and women but they were lost when a very tidy cleaner threw them away.

GRITTTAKETEN (formerly VIOLET DELL)

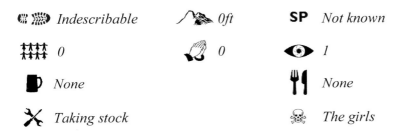

Indescribable *0ft* **SP** *Not known*

0 *0* *1*

None *None*

Taking stock *The girls*

Once popular as a picnic spot for Sunday school outings and lovers' trysts this secluded area is now visited for very different reasons since it won a measure of national notoriety in the late 1990s.

It currently bears the name of the television tough-guy and jungle survival expert, Garth Gritt. He was traversing this tract of marshland for a lone-explorer documentary when he became detached from his supporting convoy of all-terrain accommodation and catering vehicles, his cameramen, producers, sound recordists, lighting engineers, make-up artists and public relations advisers. The great man became delirious, lost and starving for several days until he was found by the Fairy Troop of a local girls' folk-dancing club who were out gathering wild flowers to decorate a bower for their Fairy Queen, Mavis Burge, aged nine.

It was Mavis who first spotted Garth; he was in tears and cowered as she approached. The other little girls quickly gathered round and gently led the stumbling hero of many desert and jungle adventures to the safely of the floral bower where, revived by Cheesy Wotsits and a can of Vimto, he was shortly joined by several mothers summoned by excited daughters, their menfolk all being away from the area on a lucrative road construction contract.

At this point, Mavis's mother, Mrs Belinda Burge, in her role as leader of both the Bluebell and Primrose Fairies, took command of the situation and in due course the intrepid traveller was restored to the television crew and resumed filming.

Long after Gritt and his team had left, a passing stranger found an abandoned film-maker's clapper-board still bearing the words 'Gritt Take Ten' and, believing this to be the name of the place, propped it up in a bush. As a result it did, over time, become its name and now many people speak of 'Gritttaketen' without knowing why.

Above: Three of the Fairy Troop who rescued
the lost and starving survival expert Garth Gritt.

SAN FRANCISCO

♢♢ *Unrecorded*   /▴▴ *0ft*   **SP** *Incalculable*

♣♣ *0*   🙏 *0*   👁 *0*

⚏ *None*   🍴 *None*

✕ *None*   ☠ *Boredom*

An air of tragedy hangs over this strangely named and now deserted site that once held the hopes of a whole community of Cambridge intellectuals in the 1960s. Calling themselves the Flower Children of the Fens, they left the city's congestion and their lives of luxurious anxiety to seek love and simplicity. For weeks they traversed ditch and dyke, mere and marsh, chanting 'Hare Krishna, Hare Krishna' in search of their promised land. At last their exhausted leader, Denzil Peterkin, a.k.a. Celestial Prophet, collapsed on a tuffet of twitch and declared this to be San Francisco.

While the men set about building rude shelters for their first night, the women went out to find food and returned to report there was no wholefood outlet within walking distance. Denzil turned to his people and asked who among them had thought to bring food and one, Muriel Ison a.k.a. Ethereal Muriel, said she had brought seeds for the future. She showed Denzil her seeds and they were of nasturtium, marigolds, love-in-a-mist, snapdragons and various daisies. 'But it is October and we cannot sow them until Spring and even then we can't eat them,' said Denzil.

'You may eat nasturtiums,' said Muriel while admitting that a nibble of nasturtium was scarcely a hearty diet.

Despite abandoning their vegetarian principles at an early stage, this brave band of dreamers failed to survive the winter with the exception of Ethereal Muriel who told their tale in a series of dramatic letters to the editor of *Mill Road Dharma Karma Tidings* before expiring from exposure and malnutrition in a private hospital in Cambridge paid for by her father, an armaments manufacturer and patron of the arts.

When visiting the site of San Francisco today all you will find is a few beads, the occasional guitar plectrum and a flourishing jungle of a type of tall weed found nowhere else on the fen.

Above: The tall weed found nowhere else on the fen.

WARM PONDS

🐾 👣 *Muddy*   ⛰ *Variable*   **SP** *Variable*

🧑‍🤝‍🧑 *Variable*   🙏 *Variable*   👁 *5*

🔋 *The Muddy Mary*   🍴 *The Mud Pie*

⚒ *Mud mining*   ☠ *Mud*

This exciting new tourist destination came into existence only very recently and is the scene of urgent activity owing to fears that it may disappear as unexpectedly as it first appeared.

 We cannot guarantee that Warm Ponds will still be in this location when the traveller follows this itinerary.

To understand the significance of Warm Ponds it must be placed in the context of the long-established Warm Bucket Cult.[*]

For centuries it had been thought that very few bona fide Warm Buckets existed, but since the publication of *Who's Who in Grunty Fen* more people have admitted to owning one and isolated examples of Warm Buckets are now found scattered across the entire region. Typically a family have harboured a Warm Bucket in an outhouse, handing it down through the generations. These buckets are seldom found within a family habitation because they have a curious sickly odour like hyacinths which some people find disagreeable. In the words of Mrs Irene Girdlestone, who keeps her family's Warm

---

[*]*For an account of the Warm Bucket phenomenon published before the discovery of Warm Ponds, see* Who's Who in Grunty Fen *pp43-46.*

Bucket in a well-ventilated back porch, 'It's like liquorice bootlaces – you can have too much of a good thing.'

A survey before the discovery of Warm Ponds suggested there were up to nine such buckets in existence, one of the most famous being at Grunty Fen where the owner, Dennis, keeps it in what he calls his Miscellaneous Shed. Those who have had access to this bucket report it contains about a half-gallon of a dark, shining, glutinous substance which never freezes, even in the hardest frost, is always viscous and radiates a constant warmth.

Not only the nature but the origin of these Warm Buckets had always been a mystery but it now seems possible that the warm substance emerges naturally from the fen soil, although probably not at the location now known as Warm Ponds because local people familiar with that area declare it had never been seen there until very recently. We are left with the possibility that there are, or have been, other, temporary sources of the substance elsewhere.

In the past, owners of Warm Buckets were reluctant to share their small supplies with others but now the substance is freely available in a public place, albeit well off the beaten track. The fortunate few who have dipped a vessel in one of the five small warm ponds and carried away a quantity are experimenting with it, but scientists in Cambridge, at the National Physical Laboratory and the Massachusetts Institute of Technology are still baffled, despite reports that the substance has allegedly cured the Green Flux, the disease which has cursed fen folk for centuries. As things now stand, Warm Ponds is a minuscule version of a healing spa or even Lourdes.

Meanwhile, entrepreneurs are investing in technology to harness the power of Warm Buckets and possibly free mankind from its quest for safe sources of energy.

Right: A feathered visitor to Grunty Fen bathes his feet in a Warm Bucket.

Above: A Warm Pond which has come up under a patch of the strap-like plant Doctors' Garters (see The Customs and Folklore of Grunty Fen *p79).*

UPPER AND LOWER DRAYNE

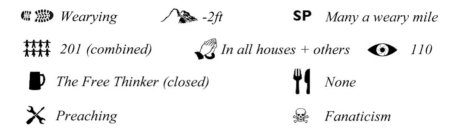

Wearying   *-2ft*   **SP** *Many a weary mile*

201 (combined)   *In all houses + others*   *110*

The Free Thinker (closed)   *None*

Preaching   *Fanaticism*

Much as the United States has Dallas and Fort Worth, Hungary has Buda and Pest and India has Hyderabad and Secunderabad, so our own dear Fens has the twin settlements of Upper and Lower Drayne, generally known as The Draynes.

Often referred to as the powerhouse of fen pulpits, the Draynes were once diametrically opposed in matters of religion. Upper Drayne believed that since the Heavenly Hierarchy had a King, all other ranks from archangel to angels through to seraphim, cherubim and saints should logically be known as royal dukes, dukes, marquises, earls and barons, or their female equivalents. The only division among the Upper Drayne faithful concerned life peers: some were certain heaven had life peers and others saying this was impossible because to be in heaven a life peer would have to be a dead peer and a peer cannot be both alive and dead at the same time.

Meanwhile, the religious community in neighbouring Lower Drayne said that since their holy books made no mention of dukes, marquises, marchionesses or any other classification of nobility they could not exist in heaven.

To which the Upper Drayners angrily responded, 'Then why have a king? You can't have a king with no nobility.'

To which the Lower Drayners replied that archangels, angels, seraphim and cherubim were all mentioned in the book, but the Upper Drayners replied that there was no mention of saints so how could saints exist in heaven if they had to be mentioned to exist?

To which the Lower Drayners said it was all a matter of faith but the Upper Drayners pointed out that the Lower Drayners had several archbishops in their village but there was no mention of archbishops, bishops or even curates and lay readers in the book so where did they all come from?

The relationship between the two villages became so bitter that even children were forbidden to play with the other side and inter-marriage was held to be invalid. Fist fights involving archbishops and the laity were commonplace.

Quite suddenly all this antagonism was swept away. On the night of November 5th 1954, people in both villages witnessed a miraculous illumination in the eastern skies like the Pillar of Fire seen by the Israelites. Later generations realised that this had been a firework display in Ely but by that time the 'miraculous' sign had long been accepted as a heavenly command to live in peace together.

Since then the two have combined systems so that all archbishops are also royal dukes, all archangels are prophets and so on. Life peers are believed to be in limbo.

Visitors should linger to sample the multitude of sermon styles to be heard both in the domestic shrines and public places of worship. You will be invited to make a contribution when the alms bucket comes around.

 Money is not welcome because there is nowhere to spend it. Food is preferred or, in the case of the entire circuit of chapels devoted to the Anglo-Saxon divine St Weedram, a whisky miniature is welcome (single malt; proprietary blends may offend).

Above: Even the humblest of constructions can be a place of worship in The Draynes, although individual congregations may be small.

♦ ITINERARY FOUR ♦

New Luton – East Pole – Dirty Corner

This page is blank for you to draw your own map of the route.

NEW LUTON

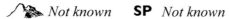 Holy   Not known   **SP** Not known    52 (est.)

 The Oratory of the Little Sisters of Perpetual Availability (unorthodox)   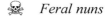 The Oratory

The Three Nuns Cocktail Bar & Cabaret (no pole dancing on Good Friday)   Get Stuffed

 Plunder Truck   Feral nuns

At the time of writing, this is the latest arrival among the area's many villages and the manner of its arrival is unique: down the centuries fen folk have well been used to villages coming and going, appearing and disappearing, but New Luton is the first to be created by a quirk of 21st-century technology.

It was in April 2002 that a convoy of six low-loaders set out from Bedfordshire each bearing a mobile bungalow destined for a luxury holiday camp on the East Coast. They never arrived.

One Nathan 'Noddy' Bender drove the leading vehicle and trusted his GPS device to plot his route to Scratby. His equally trusting colleagues in the other five low-loaders followed him all day, never questioning the directions beamed to them by an orbiting satellite, even when the roads became increasingly narrow and less frequented by other traffic. Eventually the entire cavalcade of bungalows became wedged up a muddy lane too narrow for turning. It was only then that Nathan and his mates first suspected their guiding gadget had a glitch.

Night fell. The six drivers and their mates dossed down in the bungalows still perched on their lorries and wondered where they were. Lacking a signal for their mobile telephones they decided to split up and try to find signs of civilization.

It was Clayton Wellnye, a driver's mate, who stumbled on one of the caravan nunneries of the Little Sisters of Perpetual Availability, a religious order which, according to local legend, continues to terrorise a huge area as they range the fens on their Vespa motor scooters enslaving defenceless men to perform general duties at their scattered temporary nunneries, always one step ahead of bishops and the police.

When the detachment of the Little Sisters who were ravaging that immediate area heard Clayton speak of how a dozen young men and a supply of desirable accommodation was less than a mile away, they readily responded to his call for help. Led by Mother Alacrity, they reached the stranded convoy and instantly struck up warm relationships with the truckers. Like Ulysses and his lotus eaters, the men were bewitched, beguiled and entrapped by the wayward and rapacious sisters.

Among the Little Sisters were several – including Sister Lubricity, Sister Hilarity and Sister Hospitality – who in their earlier lives had frequented truckers' cafes and overnight bedding facilities. This, plus fervent prayers and time spent in HGV cabs, gave them sufficient grasp of the controls to manoeuvre six huge low-loaders out of the lane after the truckers had helped them remove the little bungalows. Months later, the empty low-loaders were found on a remote woodland road near Brize Norton with nothing to connect them to their journey from the Fens.

As for their drivers, they have cut all ties with their former families in the Luton area and have become lay brothers under Mother Alacrity and her ladies. Repeated attempts by bishops and police to approach the nunnery have been so vigorously repelled that they have now withdrawn in despair.

 Visitors are urged not to approach the nunnery although it is possible to glimpse it from a knoll half a mile away and heavy metal rock music can be heard on religious festival days. Gentlemen should never go alone but always be accompanied by a sturdy lady.

Above: The only known photograph of New Luton.

EAST POLE

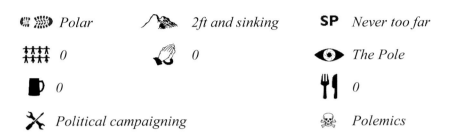

🐾🐾 *Polar* ⛰️ *2ft and sinking* **SP** *Never too far*

♨️ *0* 🙏 *0* 👁️ *The Pole*

🍺 *0* 🍴 *0*

⚔️ *Political campaigning* ☠️ *Polemics*

Lacking rigging or sails and far-sundered from the sea, there stands on a grassy fenland plain a monumental mainmast reputedly taken from a Royal Naval warship once sailed by Norfolk-born Admiral Lord Nelson. It was planted here by fervent campaigners for regional independence who reasoned that if there was a North Pole and a South Pole it was only just and logical to have an East Pole.

Visible for many miles around and a rallying point for secessionist East Anglians, it flies the brown flag of the movement on days devoted to the memory of Queens Boadicea and Etheldreda, Hereward the Wake, Coke of Holcombe, Benjamin Britten, Thomas Gainsborough, Tom Paine, John Constable, Stephen Fry, Lester Piggott and other worthies. Her Majesty the Queen, as owner of a huge area of Norfolk, has been invited to become patron but has so far failed to respond.

A vast mass of rusting corrugated iron and other ferrous materials have been heaped around and hammered into the base of the pole both as votive offerings and an attempt to create a strong magnetic field to rival that of the North and South poles.

On Nelson's birthday a great crowd numbering many dozens of men and women keen to sever ties with England assemble at the

East Pole to chant 'The East is Ours and the East is Brown' before feasting on Newmarket sausages, Cromer crabs, Yarmouth bloaters, fen celery, fen carrots and Orford oysters washed down with beer from Southwold and Bury St Edmunds.

On the political front, the East Anglian Independence Party has already seized control of a parish council in Suffolk.

Above: A view up East Pole showing some of the votive offerings. These may be bought from the East Pole Gift Shop (open alternate Saturdays). Savvy travellers arrive early to be at the front of the queue to borrow the hammer.

DIRTY CORNER

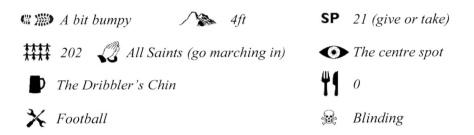

A bit bumpy   4ft   **SP**   21 (give or take)

202   All Saints (go marching in)   The centre spot

The Dribbler's Chin   0

Football   Blinding

Lucky the questing traveller who arrives at this otherwise unremarkable village when the Glow-Worms are to play the Ever-Readies. It is on such a moonlit and magical night that one of the strangest spectacles the fens have to offer takes place: floodlit football without floodlights.

Football is the lifeblood of Dirty Corner. Even its name springs not from poor hygiene but from a notorious incident in a game of football shortly after the Tumbling Tompkinsons first settled here. (Let us not venture yet again into that shameful episode. As Mrs Eleanor Barcham, who was so closely involved in the deplorable incident and its appalling aftermath, said on her deathbed: 'Best let bygones be bygones.')

The Tumbling Tompkinsons are acrobats who tired of their nomadic life and sought somewhere their children could gain an education. To their dismay none of the local schools challenged young minds and football occupied most of the curricula.

The Tompkinson children attended Dolt Primary and passed all their football examinations with ease, thanks partly to the tumbling and acrobatic skills passed on by their parents. Cashing in on their children's success, the Tomkinson clan formed a football team to win the friendship of neighbouring settlements.

But arranging matches during the winter football season was difficult. The Tompkinsons and their neighbours worked hard at their trades during every daylight hour; having renounced show-business, the Tompkinsons grasped any earning opportunity and after sunset it was too dark to play football.

Undaunted, they challenged rival teams to play by candlelight. This was a brave try but impractical: whenever a player dribbled down the wing at speed the air blew out his candle, and hot wax was an additional problem in goalmouth scrambles.

It was not long before candles were replaced by battery-powered flashlights, a brief experiment with hurricane lamps having been abandoned after slopped paraffin was ignited by one of the players' dropped cigarette butts and burned down the pavilion killing a dozen in-lay Rhode Island Reds. The site is now used for fire-worship funerals and memorial barbeques.

The use of flashlights has revolutionised the sport, and now crowds come from great distances to see the spellbinding spectacle of almost invisible players scanning the darkness to catch another player in their beams.

Torch-lit football has something in common with golf in that it is plagued by the frequency of lost balls. Boys searching the bushes to find balls toss them back into the game so that play continues for ten or fifteen minutes before the players realise they are using two or even three balls. On one occasion a game continued for twenty-one minutes with no balls at all. A committee of the FFF (Flashlit Football Federation) has been tasked with devising a set of rules to regulate these problems but a proposal to use luminous balls has already been rejected on the grounds that it would 'take all the fun out of it'. As an interim measure the boys in the under-17 teams have invited sporting girls to help them look for balls in the bushes.

Above: This dramatic shot of the burning pavilion was taken by Samuel 'Snapper' Wildgoose. The heat was so intense that it melted his lens cap.

 This space has been left blank for you to record match highlights.

♦ OTHER PLACES OF INTEREST ♦

The Fortresses – The Zoo –
The Great Central Swamp and The Pylon People –
Retard Hall – Great Cambridge University

THE FORTRESSES

Exploring mighty bastions is not only for tourists at the Tower of London, Windsor or other castles. When the Nazi terror threatened these islands early in the Second World War an imposing chain of a dozen massive concrete defensive structures was erected around Grunty Fen. This 20th-century equivalent of the Cinque Ports remains intact and provides a poignant pilgrimage for visitors.

For a small fee, local lads will show you the famous Spam Pillbox where an immense stockpile of canned meat was found after the war. The Spam itself was the foundation of many a sumptuous Christmas dinner in the days of rationing but none now remains. However, your guide will show you the curious mosses and other growths on the walls spattered with Spam when long-out-of-date cans exploded, reverberations spreading far across the fen in a ghostly echo of warfare.

Another of the pillboxes remains popular with courting couples and your guide will point out the many graphic illustrations on the interior walls. A third pillbox has been taken over by the Women's Institute who have transformed it into The Tudor Tea Rooms where they sell brawn horns, the delicacy for which the area is famous (see this volume p24 and *The Authorised Guide to Grunty Fen* p69). All profits go to the church air-freshener fund.

Apart from two pillboxes which have become the hereditary seats of the Flack and Gridley dynasties, the other concrete emplacements remain unrestored behind barbed wire and brambles. It is worth paying your guide to find a way through and enable you to enter a fortress that invites a sense of awe as you share the same space where fearless fen forefathers spent dark nights plotting Hitler's downfall and, as numerous graffiti testify, playing dominoes.

Above: Wise tourists buy their food only from W.I. outlets such as the Tudor Tea Rooms. For further details about the menu, see pp24-25.

THE ZOO

Occasionally in your travels about this ever-intriguing area, and especially in the small hours of the morning, you may hear a most baleful howling as of a soul in the torments of Hell. This is the ackerack, the only remaining denizen of the Fenland Zoo apart from the rats and rabbits; all other exhibits have died of diseases in the past thirty years leaving only this lone ackerack.

Vaguely reminiscent of the hyena with hints of warthog and sloth, this mud-coloured mammal is not only the last survivor of the zoo but also probably the last ackerack in the world. Zoo records do not state where the creature was found in the wild or when, so no-one knows its age or natural habitat. It is believed to be female but no-one has ever got close enough to be sure. What is certain is that zoologists have found no other examples of the species anywhere on any continent.

Its bleak concrete compound is strewn with the mangled remnants of past experiments to make it feel at home – rocks, logs,

Above: The Rockery, that part of the ackerack enclosure which not only lacks greenery but also lacks an ackerack. As can be deduced from the lack of ackerack, this environment did not suit the lonely creature.

a tree and a pond – but nothing ever took its fancy.

Its keeper, Graham, feeds it the remains of his packed lunch – sardine, cheese and ham sandwiches. Zoo funds do not cover the cost of a more varied diet but the ackerack eats this unvarying fare so eagerly that Graham believes there must be a lot of bread, cheese, ham and sardines wherever he, she or it comes from.

The surmise that it is female springs from the belief that when it is in season it stays awake all night howling for a mate. Alas, its mate died many years ago from neglect because, according to Graham, 'no-one was much bothered with saving such an ugly creature.'

For a small gratuity Graham will make the ackerack demonstrate its sorrowful howling by poking it with a stick.

 The zoo is open most Wednesdays: Children 6p, Adults half-price. The ackerack is always grateful for any sort of food visitors are kind enough to bring specially or may happen to find in their pockets.

 This space has been left blank for you to sketch the ackerack.

THE GREAT CENTRAL SWAMP

Readers who have seen recent television adventure documentaries and felt inspired to see the spectacle for themselves should prepare themselves for possible disappointment.

There was a time when explorers could set out into 'The Great Unknown', but sadly, the world has run out of great unknowns. The public yearns for Big Foot, the Yeti, El Dorado, unicorns, dragons, King Solomon's Mines and Shangri-la yet it is almost impossible to set foot where no-one has set foot before. Indeed, professional adventurers are at their wits' end trying to make a living. In order to attract the necessary public attention, they may resort to crossing Antarctica on a unicycle or climbing Everest on one leg.

This is a loss to the world but a gain for fenmen. Scores of travellers dependent on television fees and university grants have turned to what they have called The Great Central Swamp as the last global challenge. Until the television teams started to arrive, The Great Central Swamp was known locally as The Yewgewin, probably a corruption of 'You go in', carrying the implied 'but you don't come out.'

Ancient manuscripts preserved in Ely Cathedral endow the Yewgewin with a menagerie of serpentine monsters slithering in an evil morass. The alluring legends have captivated the present generation of television documentary makers who were welcomed with open arms by those denizens inhabiting the edges of what they learned to call The Great Central Swamp. Families who had for generations survived by making eelskin braces, belts and garters for a shrinking demand at Cambridge academic outfitters grasped the heaven-sent opportunity and became guides and souvenir sellers.

Their homes became bed and breakfast establishments catering for the demands of famous explorers, and one landlady attracted the cream of the clientele by studying their every whim. She discovered that the greatest names in the exploration business were fastidious men with heavily-hyphenated names and a preference for quilted toilet paper, lavender soap, fresh flowers and croutons in their soup; the ferociously-bearded Sir Bracken Gascoyne Berk de Barronne, hero of many perilous treks through jungles, deserts and glaciers, demands rose petals in his bath and smoked salmon for breakfast. Some of these refinements have rubbed off on the native population who until recently had never encountered table napkins or body lotion.

Above: The beauty of the Great Central Swamp is often obscured by fen mist or fog created by rotting vegetation and, tragically, lost explorers.

For their part, the television producers found The Great Central Swamp not only easy to reach from their London offices but a cheaper location than Borneo or the Amazon basin.

Old Etonians always get on well with their social inferiors so profitable friendships spring up between local fenmen offering to act as guides to the courageous gentlemen being filmed journeying into this newly fashionable Great Unknown. For the convenience of the hardy pioneers, the guides have built simple staging posts where weary travellers can find comfortable beds and simple meals cooked by local ladies who guard the secret of dry pathways avoiding an unpleasant trudge through the mire.

This area has become so popular with explorers that little fen lanes become clogged with camera teams' 4x4s and one local council is considering a booking system to avoid more than four expeditions at any one time. But such is the television viewers' appetite for the rugged lives of great men who endure physical and mental hardships in their search for knowledge that such a system is thought unlikely to stem the flood. Several expeditions are now racing to complete the first complete circumnavigation of the swamp and others set out in great numbers in search of the legendary lost civilisation of the Pylon People (see next page).

 Ordinary tourists are advised that it is possible to take a pleasant trek across the swamp with a picnic lunch served by Mrs Griffin at Bide-a-wee, the bungalow next to the main expedition departure point.

THE PYLON PEOPLE

Here we have an astonishing and mysterious folk legend for which there is solid documentary evidence. That said, we must question the evidence of our own eyes, just as photographs of the Loch Ness Monster are now seen as fakes.

Taking the evidence at face value would mean that somewhere in the wilderness of the Great Central Swamp there exists a full-size National Grid electricity pylon lying on its side. It can be seen in a photograph taken with a box camera by the Rev. Charles Cleverley in the late 1930s. Despite the double exposure it is possible to see the huge structure lying across what seems to be a dried-up river bed.

No other pylons are to be seen; the Great Central Swamp does not lie on the route of any projected or redundant power line and is in no way connected to the National Grid. So who put the pylon there, how and why?

This mystery has stumped some of the best brains in archaeology and engineering; only the anthropologists, ethnographers and sociologists have offered any sort of logical theory. While the archaeologists and engineers compare the feat of moving this huge and heavy structure with the achievement of the builders of Stonehenge in moving the large Blue Stones from the faraway Preseli Mountains, the sociologists, ethnographers and anthropologists have created a theory involving an entire civilization which arose and vanished in less than a century. This race they call the Pylon People.

Proponents of the Pylon People at first believed their culture originated in ancient Egypt where pharaonic dynasties erected lofty obelisks to their greater glory. But if such a race ever existed, where are they now and why did they put the pylon where they did?

Opponents of this pharaonic theory point out that there are no other traces of the Pylon People yet evidence for the Beaker People is found all over Europe. Cases of civilizations rising and falling on a single site in a short space of time are vanishingly rare.

If the so-called Pylon People moved the pylon, where did they find it or how did they make it and, if their inspiration was the Egyptian obelisk, why does it lie on its side with nothing to suggest that it ever stood erect?

The single source of evidence to answer all these questions that has been resolutely ignored by all these experts lies in a few brief articles and letters published in *The Grunter* local newspaper in 1933, which was about the time that parts of the Grid were being extended or erected. The text of a sermon by the Rev. Dr Nathaniel Gravely, sometime Priest in Charge at St Judas', Grunty Fen, is printed in *The Grunter*; it quotes the Book of Ezeriah in condemning 'the wickedness at Guttering Mere'. *

The Rev. Dr Graveley called the inhabitants of Guttering Mere 'the black sheep of my flock' who 'have conspired against the power of the state and all its apparatus' to achieve 'a convenience for a few fearful souls'. In later issues correspondents take issue with Dr Gravely pointing out the Lord bade Noah to build an ark 'and them living at Guttering Mere ain't doing no more'n that'.

Piecing together other hints taken from reports and letters it is possible to construct a convincing explanation for the pylon. The clinching evidence comes in a public notice published in 1933 signed by the chief engineer of the Central Electricity Board in which he offers a reward for any evidence leading to the recovery of 'the

Guttering Mere no longer exists, having been consumed by the fen, and should not be confused with the village of Guttering which, at time of writing, is still in existence.

82

Above: The Rev. Cleverley's famous double-exposure photograph.

whole or any parts of pylon GRY-399-B 15,000v missing from a delivery convoy of lorries on or about the weekend of July 11-12.' A later public announcement begged for help in tracing one of the lorry drivers.

Some months later a local celebrity, Mrs Elsa Mayhew of The Bull, Grunty Fen – area champion in both the darts and dominoes leagues – was invited to formally open 'Guttering Mere's new bridge' by breaking a bottle of barley wine 'on the girders'. Mrs Mayhew, who was also captain of the mixed tug-o'-war and the Scant Ladies All-In Wrestling teams, was reported as celebrating the fact that it had become possible for 'a frail lady' to cross the flooded river between Guttering Mere and East Muck.

As neither of these villages now exist – not uncommon where communities come and go over the centuries as the fen 'spits and sucks', according to local people – then the whereabouts of the bridge-cum-pylon, the river it once crossed and the alleged Pylon People must forever be a mystery.

One other artefact remains, now in the possession of Scowl Parish Council: a weatherworn noticeboard setting out the tolls for using 'the new bridge' – tolls mainly payable not in pence but in fresh produce. It is just possible to decipher *One infant in arms – one lettuce* and *All darts and dommies teams – free.*

If this is the origin of the Pylon People then they presumably moved away when the river and the tolls ceased to flow. But how these simple country folk moved hundreds of tons of steelwork across miles of quaking marsh remains a mystery. Perhaps, after all, they were descended from the ancient Egyptians who built the pyramids and raised the obelisks of Memphis.

 This space has been left blank for you to record the location of the pylon should you see it. Please notify Miss Edwards at Grunty Fen Post Office Stores: telephone Grunty Fen 1.

RETARD HALL

Wherever you wander you are bound at one point to see, stark upon the horizon, what at first looks like a giant hand or gaunt fingers clawing at the sky. This is Retard Hall. As you draw nearer it becomes clear that the fingers are ruinous chimney stacks rising from a crumbling chaos of roofs, towers and walls.

The present mistress of Retard Hall does not mince her words when describing the ancestral home. 'We call it a stately home because it's in such a state,' Hatshepsut Calne-Foley-Retard tells visitors. Pointing to the way that large patches of Edwardian cement rendering have flaked away from the ancient red brick beneath, she declares, 'My house looks as if it has a horrible skin disease,' and the damage does for all the world look like livid wounds suppurating under gigantic scurf. But this is the least of the Hon. Hattie's problems.

For centuries this once-noble edifice has been sinking into the fen and successive ancestors have been obliged to pile new storeys on top of the submerged Anglo-Saxon, Plantagenet, Tudor and Jacobean layers. In addition, the present central structure is unstable. Concentric rings of tottering, single-storey lean-to annexes buttress the core but even they are subsiding under the weight of billiard tables and the private museum boasting several ancient Egyptian sarcophagi brought home by her father, a keen amateur archaeologist (hence Hatshepsut's first name). Miraculously, the tall Tudor chimney stacks remain more or less intact, pointing skyward like arthritic fingers or, as she once put it, 'like newly extracted molars'.

The art deco ballroom added by her grandmother houses a profitable mushroom farm and Hattie has launched several other fund-raising schemes now that income from the Retard estate has dwindled as the land steadily sinks and becomes impossible to farm.

Her latest idea, the 'HattiMac', already employs a dozen fen ladies in a factory set up in the long gallery. Here they convert old belted mackintoshes of the sort worn by all fenmen into luxury gardening garments for keen lady gardeners seeking the 'shabby chic' look. After the old macs have had a good rinse, the ladies set about fitting pockets to take trowels, secateurs, shears, pruning hooks; tea, cocktail and other drinks flasks; sou'westers, hand cream and even folding saws, sickles and scythes. This product is aimed at ladies who, like Hattie herself, have large gardens to maintain and do not wish constantly to make the long journey back to the tool shed.

Hattie may be seen modelling her invention in advertisements in *The Lady, Country Life* and other upmarket magazines under the slogan 'HattiMac – The Shed You Can Wear'. She has made it clear in her sales literature that her coats are designed for fit countrywomen able to carry the weight of a fully loaded mac rather than for delicate suburban gardeners. Even so, she has received a few complaints from ladies who found Hattie's macs too heavy, including one lady in Gloucestershire who fell over in her wisteria pergola and lay there unable to rise for several hours until her butler rang the dinner gong and noted her absence. Learning a lesson from this sad event, Hattie now fits a variety of alarm systems in each mac.

Hattie is also trying to attract more paying visitors by developing her garden in two different ways. She has persuaded a Cambridge scientist to examine the possibility of harnessing the remarkable scum on her pond as a source of energy. Hattie's scum forms a solid six-inch layer twice a day in summer and once in winter; she sometimes has to help her gardener take it off in a sodden heap to be dumped on the bog at the end of the garden in a bid to extend the cultivable area of her property. Hattie envisions vast industrial reservoirs covered in her super-scum and constantly harvested for a power station or direct conversion to fuel.

Meanwhile, her second garden scheme involves planting a Fen Botanical Garden featuring all the wild plants noted in *The Authorised Guide to Grunty Fen, Who's Who in Grunty Fen* and *The Customs and Folklore of Grunty Fen* plus others unique to her corner of the Fens such as those detailed below.

PLANTS UNIQUE TO THE RETARD HALL ESTATE

Common Stenchwort (*odorifera vulgaris*): An unspectacular daisy with an unbearable scent used to deter witches and burglars. Highly poisonous.

Dainty Sludge Bells (*campanula cloaca*): Used as a buttonhole by confirmed bachelors who wish to stay that way.

Leaping Leper (*pariah vaultatus*): A rapidly growing highly poisonous climber with leaves that keep rotting and falling off.

Virgin's Lust Grass (*virgixmibus concupisiens fescue*): A legendary aphrodisiac favoured by young men when courting.

Scabs and Bruises (*contusion sanguinarice*): A low-growing ground-cover plant that thrives at the edges of septic tanks and looks exactly like its traditional name. Highly poisonous.

Lucifer's Tail (*unknown to botanists*): A whip-like highly poisonous spike of barbed thorns which tears the flesh of passers-by.

Left: Hatshepsut Calne-Foley-Retard models her creation.

To complement the HattiMac there is the HattiHat, which as well as providing sun protection is ideal for transporting coilable items such as ropes, twine, chains, etc.

With every purchase, Hattie includes liquorice bootlaces and a string of pearls 'in case the bishop calls. He loves liquorice bootlaces!'

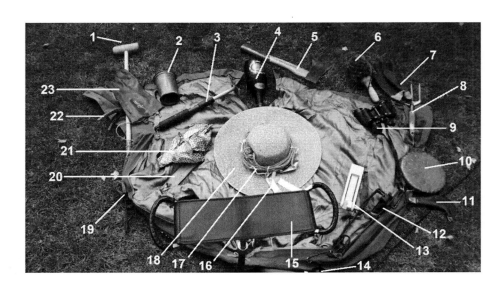

As can be seen from the picture on the facing page, each HattiMac and HattiHat can be stocked with various items to suit the purchaser's needs but typically will hold the following:

1   Mallet

2   Tankard

3   Cuttlefish hoe

4   Non-vintage sparkling wine

5   Axe

6   Fettling brush

7   Heavy duty glove (R)

8   Hand fork

9   Binoculars

10   Dinner gong (non-folding)

11   Whitby billhook (folding)

12   Stem-clumper

13   Bird scarer / distress alarm

14   Telephone receiver

15   Shooting stick

16   Emergency bandage

17   Rope

18   Sun hat

19   Channel-cutter

20   Rasp

21   Distinctive handkerchief / distress flag

22   Ring girdler

23   Heavy duty glove (L)

GREAT CAMBRIDGE UNIVERSITY

Great Cambridge University was founded in 1957 by self-styled 'Professor' Barry 'Danny' Daniel. The institution opened in the city of Cambridge and offered correspondence courses in ballroom dancing, chiropody, topiary, dental hygiene, ventriloquism, cricket score-keeping and hymn-writing.

When the University of Cambridge learned of this other university, based at 87 Sebastopol Villas in its own city, the Vice-Chancellor acted to force Danny out of business, but succeeded only in forcing him out of town.

Danny, after many years cycling around the city as a life assurance agent, was a powerful pedaller. He loaded his university into two strong cardboard boxes on to the pillion rack of his Hercules and hit the A10 just ahead of the proctors' arrival at No.87.

Alas, on reaching the Stretham crossroads Danny was struck a mortal blow when a sugar beet dropped like a cannonball from a lorry speeding towards the Ely Sugar Refinery. Local tourist guide and verger of St Judas' parish church, Dennis, heard the academic's last words: 'Don't let me students down.' It was only when Dennis, having claimed salvage rights, reached his home and examined the boxes that he realised the import of these words.

Hitherto, Dennis's best academic subject at primary school some 30 years earlier had been the period on the timetable called 'quiet time' at which his teacher, Miss Turkentine, said he excelled. He was also proud that he left school able to spell 'phlegm' and 'diarrhoea'. Now a sense of duty to the dead Danny, together with a determination not to let an earner slip through his fingers, obliged Dennis to ransack everything he had learned at school before completing his education at the age of 11.

Overnight this master of quiet time became vice-chancellor, professor, tutor and bursar of an international educational enterprise specialising in students in some of the further-flung corners of the old British Empire. Dennis found he had clients in St Kitts and Nevis, British Honduras, Fiji, Baffin Land, Swaziland and Cox's Bazaar, plus a host of eager topiarists in Tuvalu.

On the advice of his friend Miss Edwards, church organist and proprietrix of the Grunty Fen Post Office Stores, he arranged for mail to be redirected to his home, a converted Edwardian railway carriage. Soon, fees began to flow, taking the form of every currency from cowrie shells to zlotys which his friend Miss Edwards declined to touch, deeming it to be 'filthy foreign money'. She declared that, since most foreigners wore loin cloths and loin cloths had no pockets, 'you don't know where it's been'.

With the money came essays for him to mark and the need to find new work for students. He rummaged in the cardboard boxes for something appropriate but, inevitably, students hoping for instructions on the quick step received a detailed guide to the use of descant in hymnody and other students keen on clipping toenails learned how to shape a privet cockerel.

Responding to a huge heap of complaints was a slow process. Although Dennis was well equipped with several veteran typewriters retrieved from skips and dumps, none of them worked perfectly; it was necessary for a single letter to be produced on three different machines. First he set out the main structure of a letter by typing on a machine that was good at punctuation. Then a second machine did the capital letters and finally a third machine filled in the gaps with the main text. Dennis sometimes worked in the words 'phlegm' or 'diarrhoea' just to show off his learning which served only to baffle a student whose native tongue was Croat or Urdu and had difficulty with English anyway.

After a few weeks of sleepless anxiety, Dennis sold the university for £5 to the most sophisticated couple in the village, Honey Brite (née Norah Merchant) and Inigo Haycock, retired holiday camp redcoats, who hoped to augment their income from writing verses for greetings cards at £5 a thousand. In their care and after a bumpy start involving a confusion between flying and frying and between mixing cocktails and concrete, they now offer courses in basic puppetry, pig-slaughtering for beginners and bobble hats for all occasions.

Honey and Inigo have renamed their asbestos Tudor bungalow 'Great Cambridge University' and flanked the front door with two huge vertical rolls of faulty linoleum painted grey to look like the west end of King's College Chapel. The Vice-Chancellor of the University of Cambridge and the Dean of King's have long since abandoned hope of doing anything about it.

Above: Great Cambridge University

INDEX AND PICTURE CREDITS

Index

A10, the 25, 90
Abbs, Mrs Victoria 20
Academy of Dance & the Thespian
    Arts, Bludd (ad.) 22
accommodation 20
ackerack 76
Alacrity, Mother 67
Amazon basin 79
Anderson shelters 12
Anne Hathaway's Cottage 53
Apache Wells 12
Arizona 12
Armiger, Makepeace Daunt 5
Baffin Land 91
Bar Behind Bars 21
Barronne,
    Bracken Gascoyne Berk de Sir, 79
Beaker People 82
Bedford 20
Bedfordshire 18, 66
Beijing 1
Bender, Nathan 'Noddy' 66
Bethlehem Asylum for the
    Criminally Confused 52
Bigfoot 78
BIGO 25
Bitter Frogspite 24
bloaters 70
Bludd 22
Borneo 79
Brighton 8
Brite, Honey 92
British Honduras 91
Britten, Benjamin 69
Brize Norton 67
buckets, ladies' evening 27
Buda 62
Buddhism, Tibetan 35
Builders' Arms, The (PH) 52
Bull, The (PH) 83
Burge, Mavis (Fairy Queen) 55

Burge, Mrs Belinda 56
Bury St Edmunds 70
bus travel 16-20
Bustard (birds)
    Great 1, 2; Lesser, Medium, Small 2
Bustard (family), the 39
Cabbage Club, The 49
Calamity Gulch 12
Calne-Foley-Retard, Hatshepsut 85
Cambridge 7, 25, 52, 57, 58, 60, 79, 90
    University Library 53
    University 90, 92
Canard Flambé aux Deux Jambeaux,
    Brasserie du (R) 34
candlelight, football by 72
Carrion Thrush 2
Central Electricity Board 82
Chelmsford 20
Chicky-Chunks 34
Cinque Ports, 74
Cleverley, Charles, The Rev. 81
Common Stenchwort 87
Constable, John 69
coprolite 13
cosmetics corporation 44
Costa Esmeralda 49
Country Life 86
Cox's Bazaar 91
crabs, 70
Cromer 70
Craven family, the 39
Crown and Anchorite, The (PH) 37
Cruel Winter 27, 45
Cursed, family the 39; Mrs Enid 39
Dainty Sludge Bells 87
Dallas 62
Daniel,
    Barry 'Danny' 'Professor' 90
Dank 1, 7
Darlington 5
Deadman's Daisies 24

Index

Dearie Me 52
delicacies 24
Demonic Druids, Chapel of 34
Dennis 8, 60, 90
Dense 22
Devil's Bladderwort 24
Devil's Drove 47
Devil's Pittance 31, 38
Dick, 'Doomsday' 44
Dirty Corner 71
Doctors' Garters 61
Dodge Fen 4
Dolt Primary School 71
Down Market 7; College of
    Vocational Fine Arts 18, 19
Drayne, Upper and Lower 62
Dribbler's Chin, The (PH) 71
Drudge family, the 38
Dry Bicker 20
    Wednesday (FC) 28
Dry Guttering 39
Durham Cathedral 53
Dyke, Billy 'Butlin' 12-13;
    Chenille 12-13
East Anglian Independence Party 70
East Muck 83
East Pole 69
Edwards, Miss 8, 91
eelskin belts 78; boot/shoe laces 26;
    braces 78; garters 45, 78; hat 45
El Dorado 78
Ely, city 8; 63
    Cathedral 78
    Sugar Refinery 90
Equal Rights Restaurant (R) 52
Ever-Readies, The (FC) 71
Ezeriah, Book of 82
Fairfen 36, 38
Fairies, Bluebell and Primrose 55-56
Fancies Factory 24
Fearful, Thrussell, The Very Rev. 39

Fen Botanical Garden 79
Fenland and Anglia Oriental Steam
    Navigation Co. 5, 7
Fenland Zoo 76
Fen O'Clock Rock 49
fertiliser 13, 27, 28
Festering-in-the-Heaps 12
Fiji 91
Flack, dynasty 75; Reuben 48
Flashlit Football Federation 72
Flower Children of the Fens 57
fly hats 27
Flying Hat, The (PH) 45
Fly in your Soup, The (R) 45
Fortresses, The 74
Fort Worth 62
Foul Fowl 2
Free Thinker, The (PH) 62
Fry, Stephen 69
Funeral Rook 2
Fun Fair,
    Gudgeon's Super Colossal 38
Gainsborough, Thomas 69
Get Stuffed (R) 66
Gibbets, The 34
Girdlestone, Mrs Irene 59
Gloat 38
Gloucestershire 86
Glow-Worms, The (FC) 71
Golden Galloper 36, 39
Good Grief 42
Good Riddance, The, (PH) 31
Good Thrashing 38
Graham (Zoo keeper) 76
Graveley, Nathaniel, The Rev. Dr 82
Great Cambridge University 90
Great Central Swamp, The 78
Great Yarmouth 12, 70
Green Flux 20, 60
Gridley, dynasty 75; Mrs 31
Griffin, Mrs 80

Index

Grinders family, the 29
Grit 49
Gritt, Garth 55
Gritttaketen 55
Growner, Eustace 26
Grudge, Great and Little 8
Grunter, The 82
Grunty Fen 1, 60, 83, 88
  Academicals (FC) 28
  Post Office Stores 8, 91
Gudgeon, Ma 38
Guild of Sanitary Inspectors' Hall 15
Guttering 82
Guttering Mere 82
Hague, The 40
handicrafts 26
Harrowing 22
haticopter 46
HattiMac and HattiHat 86-89
Haycock, Inigo 92
Hayley, Bill 49
Heavenly Peace, Temple of 1
Her Majesty's Pleasure Hotel 20-21
Hiccup Gardens 5
High Fen 54
Highpoint 20
Hilarity, Sister 67
Hitler, Adolf 75
Holcombe, Coke of 69
Homeland Security, US Dept. of 44
Home Office 20-21
Homing Vulture 2
Hornet Tattoo & Massage Parlour,
  Dense (ad.) 22
horns, brawn 24, 74
hospital, bubonic plague isolation 43
Hospital, Cottage 16
Hospitality, Sister 67
Hove 38
Hungary 62
Hutentots 9-11

Hyderabad 62
Ilfracombe 12
Imperial Heralds,
  Universal College of 7
Isle of Wight 12
Ison, Muriel
  (aka Ethereal Muriel) 57
Israelites 63
itineraries 29
Jamaican reggae rap 42
Just Walking in the Drain 49
Killer Robin 2
King's College Chapel 92
King Solomon's Mines 78
Kukri, Nepalese 19
Lama, Daily 35
Lambert, the Rev. Morris 20
Leaping Leper 87
Le Corbusier, flats 53
leper colony 43
Limepits 9
Littlehey 20
Little Sisters of Perpetual
  Availability 67
Loch Ness Monster 81
London, Tower of 74
Lourdes 60
Lower Dregs 39
Lower Grime 32
Lubricity, Sister 67
Lucifer's Tail 87
Machu Picchu 8
maggot breeding 39-40
Maggotdonald's 38
Maggots, Elizabeth 39
Marsh Hurrier 2
Massachusetts Institute of
  Technology 60
Mayhew, Mrs Elsa 83
Memphis 84
Mendoza-Barltrop, Luigi, Lord 7

Index

Merry Maggot, The (PH) 38
Mice and Celery, The (R) 42
Mill Road Dharma Karma Tidings 58
Miscellaneous Shed 60
mouse, celery, stuffed with 42
Mucky Moses 5
Muddy Mary, The (PH) 59
Mud Pie, The 59
Museum,
   Cruel Winter 46
   East Anglian, Cultural Curiosities
   and Mouth Organs, of 12
   Salad Cream Bottles, of 12
Nagpur 1
National Grid 81
National Physical Laboratory 60
Nelson, Admiral Lord 69
New Luton 66
Newmarket 70
Nigel (bus driver) 16
Norfolk 69
Oracle, Delphic 16
Oratory, the Little Sisters of
  Perpetual Availability of 66
Orford 70
Over-60s 16, 20
Oxford Circus 1
oysters 70
Paine, Tom 69
Parliament, Members of 21
Pest 62
Peterkin, Denzil
  (aka Celestial Prophet) 57
Pevsner, Nikolaus 4
Piggott, Lester 69
Pilgrim's Feet, The (PH) 35
Pillar of Fire 63
pillboxes 74
Pious End 35
Pitts, The 35, 37
Poland 24

Poles, North and South 69
Pompidou Centre, the 53
Portmeirion 53
Prego-a-go-go! 49
Preseli Mountains 81
Privy/Pryvie/Privie, etc.,
  Chill, Dry, Dashfor, Fowl, Locknot,
  Marshland, Sticky, Water, 14
Pucker Pieshop, The (R) 32
Pylon People, The 80, 81
Queen, Boadicea 69; Etheldreda 69;
  Mother, The 40; The 69;
  Wilhelmina of the Netherlands 40
Railway, Cottages 4; Inn 4
Rank Sumps 38
Rat Dyke 38
Rat Fen Thistles (FC) 28
Reception 54
Red Sea 5
Retard Hall 85
Road Kill Pie 25
Rolling Stones, The 49
Royal Gentry Ritz Plaza, The,
  Spitehaven (ad.) 23
Rutts, East, North, South, West 8
San Francisco 57
Sapper-Trench, Louise (Lulu) 14
sausages 70
Scabs and Bruises 87
Scant 8
  Ladies All-In Wrestling Team 83
Scratby 8, 66
Scowl Parish Council 83
scum, pond 79
Secunderabad 62
sediment 28
Shangri-la 78
Shanklin 12-13
Skara Brae 53
Slimepits 9
Slug Fen 4

Index

Slurrybank Cottage, Harrowing (ad.) 22
Slutt 38
Sluvvenleigh, Low, Lower, Upper 8
Smallholding, The, Wrasp (ad.) 23
Snare 38
Society for Sanitary Reform among
   the Labouring Classes 14
Southwold 12, 70
Souvenirs 24
Spam 24, 74; Pasties 24; Pillbox 74
Spewing in the Marsh 9
Spitehaven 23
Stalag Luft 20, 48
   Interrogation Suite 20
Stalag Luft X 49
Starling, Mrs and Mr 16
Stink Pipe 1
St Judas' 82, 90
St Kitts and Nevis 91
Stonehenge 34, 81
Strangler's Spire Throttle 35
Stretham 90
Strict Perditionists For Paradise 39
Strippling, Daniel 45-46
   Time Flies, autobiography 46
St Weedram, chapels of 63
Sugar Beat Generation, the 49
Swaziland 91
Swiss Rocker, The 49
Switzerland 40
Sydney Opera Houses 53
The Lady 86
Thieves' Kitchen, The (R) 21
Three Nuns Cocktail Bar and
   Cabaret, The (PH) 66
Tombstone City 12
Tottenham Hotspur, stadium 53
triangles, knitted 27
Troy 8
Truth and Honesty, Chapel of 4
Tudor Tea Rooms, The 74

Tumbling Tompkinsons 71
Turkentine, Miss 90
Tuvalu 91
Verminstein, Merle 'Duke' 49
Virgin's Lust Grass 87
Wake, Hereward the 69
Warm Bucket cult 59
Warm Ponds 59
Watchtower, The 48
Watt, James 45
Wayfarers' bones 1
Weeping St Less 39
Wellnye, Clayton 67
West Scurfly Fen 8
whipping 32
whisks, whittled 26, 32; Whisks,
Environmentally Sustainable
   Whittled Whitewood, 33
Whistler's Lips, The (PH) 32
whistles, whittled 26, 32
wholloping 32
whopping 32
Wildgoose, Samuel 'Snapper' 72
Wight, Isle of 13
Windy Huts 16
   Rovers (FC) 28
Windsor Castle 74
Wisbech 8
Women's Institute 24, 25, 74
World War II 24, 74
Wrasp 23
Wretch 39
Writhing-cum-Wheary 39
Yeti 78
Yewgewin, The 78
Youth Club 21
Zoroastrian funerary tower 31

Picture Credits

The Author wishes to acknowledge the help given with illustrating this volume by the following individuals and organisations.

[PD = Public Domain; NK = No Known Copyright Restrictions]

The Grosvenor-Frugal Archive of Agricultural Anthropology, Tractoriana and the Coarse Arts

P7   Coat of arms by C Carman†
P29   Book covers by McCaw Press†
P83   Pylon by M Carman†
P88   Hatti-Mac and Hatti-Hat by M Carman†

Images via pixabay.com

P13   Roadsign by John Collins; Welcome wheel by Maxx Girr
P15   Toilet Image by Andrew Martin
P21   Pencil by OpenClipart-Vectors
P22   Hornet by OpenClipart-Vectors
P33   Whittling Image by LUM3N
P35   Stupas Image by Albert Dezetter
P36   Carousel horse by Jessica Christian
P40   Maggot sheds by hpgruesen (Erich Westendarp)
P43   Isolation hospital by Siggy Nowak
P44   Leper tower by falco
P47   Fly by OpenClipart-Vectors
P50   Watchtower by Hans Harbig
P54   Reception (Derelict St Crispin's) by Steven Goddard
P58   Tall weed by Valyxyz
P61   Bird on bucket by Larry White; Warm pond by 422737
P64   Church open sign by Printoid
P68   Caravans by Kevin Phillips
P70   Mast by sion maeda
P72   Burning pavilion by Pexels
P73   Football by OpenClipart-Vectors
P75   Tea room sign frame by Amber Avalona;
        Open sign by Anne-Onyme; Blackboard by Gerd Altmann
P77   Easel by OpenClipart-Vectors
P79   Great Central Swamp by werdepate (Wolfgang Zimmel)
P92   House by Steve Norris; King's College by falconimaging
Back   Wellington boot by OpenClipart-Vectors
page

Picture Credits

Opposite - The author's own photo showing him relaxing at a Grunty Fen beauty spot †

A journalist one way and another for over 60 years, Christopher South has in his time been News Editor of the Cambridge News, a widely read columnist and for the past 30-odd years a broadcaster for the BBC. Along the way he's interviewed everybody from royalty and prime ministers to a man who lived in a drain and a man who learned to read by tracing the letters on gravestones.

With the late Pete Sayers, Christopher created 500 episodes of the Dennis of Grunty Fen comedy series which ran for 17 years on the radio, bringing to life the bleak wilderness and bizarre characters who inhabit the world of Grunty Fen.

Christopher also helped to found two Cambridgeshire charities (Camtad and the Magog Trust) and ran a small charity with his wife to help poor people in Sri Lanka, for which they gave almost 500 talks. He has travelled widely, his natural curiosity about other people taking him to over 60 countries, but likes it best to be at home with his dog.

His interests include gardening, cooking, gardening, reading other people's diaries, gardening, collecting bits of famous buildings (he claims that at one time he had more of King's College Chapel than the Dean and Provost), gardening, Tottenham Hotspur and gardening.

This space has been left blank for you to record memories of your time spent in Grunty Fen.